The *Long* and the Short *of* It

The Long *and the* Short *of* It

A Practical Guide to European Versification Systems

JOSEPH A. DANE

University of Notre Dame Press
Notre Dame, Indiana

Manufactured in the United States of America

Library of Congress Cataloging-in-Publication Data

Dane, Joseph A.
The long and the short of it : a practical guide to
European versification systems / Joseph A. Dane.
p.   cm.
ISBN-13: 978-0-268-02603-5 (pbk. : alk. paper)
ISBN-10: 0-268-02603-3 (pbk. : alk. paper)
1. Versification.   2. English language—Versification.   3. Latin language—
Versification.   4. French language—Versification.   5. Poetics—Study
and teaching.   6. English poetry—Study and teaching.   I. Title.
PN1042.D35   2010
808.1094—dc22

2009053247

To *L. J.*, sailor

Contents

Acknowledgments

Inspiration for this project was provided by the many teachers who struggled to explain principles of versification to me that at least one of us, and usually both, neither understood nor with any real conviction believed. Had it not become so unfashionable after secondary school to admit such ignorance, I could have begun this book much earlier; perhaps there would have been no need of it. Among others, I thank Ron Bernard, Sidney Evans, Percival Everett, Penelope Geng, my father, various Greens, Catherine Kelley, Seth Lerer, Michaeline Mulvey, Michael Peterson, Sandra Prior, Ray Romero, Laura Scavuzzo-Wheeler and family, Margaret Russett, and the students who struggled through classes that amounted to first drafts of this book. I am also most grateful to Barbara Hanrahan and to the readers, editors, copyeditors, and designers of the University of Notre Dame Press, who have been consistently helpful, cheerful, and amusing throughout this project.

Introduction

Literary anthologies and handbooks are filled with helpful statements about versification, that is, the basic principles of verse composition. A sonnet has fourteen lines and may be Petrarchan or Shakespearean; rhymes are masculine or feminine; blank verse is unrhymed iambic pentameter. Most of my students know such things, or at least think they should, and creative writing students have no particular difficulty producing examples. Versification in foreign languages is a bit more abstract, at least for those who have not had serious language instruction. Even vague references to classical metrics are becoming rare in our classrooms, and foreign verse itself has become at best a source of quickly domesticated forms and stylistic devices. Old English contains alliteration and what are called kennings. French fixed forms are easily imitated and are treated as a variant of the Western haiku. Composing, say, a *ballade,* a *virelai,* a *sestina,* or something that looks like one, a few lines in apparent parody of *Beowulf* or even Chaucer: these are amusing and doubtless profitable exercises.

Yet looking at foreign verse in this manner omits what is a much more challenging part of that meter. A poem, even in one of these fixed forms, consists not just of a pattern of lines (how the completed poem looks), but of something more basic—those elements that constitute the line itself and its fundamental character. A French Alexandrine is not simply a line of twelve syllables, as it might be described in a verse handbook. French writers wrote these lines according to a detailed (but not overly mysterious) set of rules for determining what a syllable is and which syllable types are permitted in what line locations. A Latin hexameter is not simply a Longfellow-esque sequence of dactyls and spondees; it is constructed according to detailed (but again, not overly mysterious) rules of syllable length and accent.

The present guide is written with intelligent nonspecialists in mind, that is, poets, readers of literature, and students of literature and those who teach them. There is no reason a competent speaker of English with an interest in verse or poetry cannot easily understand the basic rules of verse composition in languages that employ the same basic alphabet. The chapters that follow will provide such readers with a working knowledge of basic principles of select European verse systems that have influenced English poets from the Renaissance to the twentieth century. The guide is practical rather than theoretical; it does not propose new theories of metrical analysis nor is it intended as a survey of scholarship in versification. Writers of English verse and students of English literature need a chance to see how English verse differs from verse in other European traditions and how those traditions have affected what today we think of as English verse. And one cannot know how Latin and French affected English unless one knows in some detail what the principles of those verse systems are.

To understand these systems requires some knowledge of what is often called prosody, that is, the minimal units of verse composition: what are the distinguishing features of syllables (e.g., stress, length) or basic rhyme types? in what cases can verse be analyzed as feet, and what are the larger elements that organize these units into lines? I will deal with larger forms (fixed forms in romance languages, lyric forms in Latin) when necessary, but I make no attempt to give any more than a cursory survey of various fixed forms, whose patterns can be readily found in other books of reference.

Students of English literature today are likely to be exposed to versification and its apparent mysteries largely in English classes. And one only has to talk to these students to realize that what now passes for general or conventional instruction in verse simply does not work. When told I was working on versification, most of my friends, whatever their level of education—high school, college, graduate— responded kindly but vaguely that they "never really got that." Even my academic colleagues, although less inclined to admit such things, prove in their discussion of verse that they never really got it either.

And no wonder. These are intelligent people; and the reason they never "got" versification is that there was likely nothing coherent in what they were taught for them to get. I have been instructed in versification since grammar school, and only because little of what I was taught stuck do I feel competent to discuss it now. There is in English a massive confusion of basic terminology, where Greek words of dubious legitimacy form our basic vocabulary of verse, where the word *long* means "accented," where style is confused with rules, and where the Great Baggy Monster of English versification—the dreaded Iambic Pentameter—is apt to leap out at any moment and smother anything that smacks of reason or clarity. Even sound attempts in English to discuss foreign verse often begin with English verse, as if the principles of English verse were familiar and well known—all in the well-intentioned attempt to show how different, say, French or Latin verse is from English. But the principles of English verse are not well known at all and the matter so little understood by students and those who teach them that this is a terrible place to begin. It would make far more sense to begin with Latin and French verse in order to understand English verse than the other way around. The basic principles of Latin and French verse are perfectly well known; most details are uncontroversial, and in some cases the basic analysis of such verse has been unchanged for centuries.

For students of grammar and literature a few generations ago, things were different from what they are today: versification was a compulsory subject. Most modern English poets, like most Victorian poets, eighteenth-century poets, early modern poets, and medieval poets, had been instructed in Latin and had had the rules for Latin verse literally beaten into them; thus no serious student of literature needed the kind of information found, say, in chapter 2 below. But the sort of exercise familiar to my own teachers (e.g., take a passage from Livy and write it in the style of Tacitus; rewrite this passage of Milton in Latin hexameters) was certainly not part of my education. Today, I know many competent classicists who struggle mightily with the basics of verse analysis. The situation is not much different in French and Italian; in my experience, those who sing these languages are often more familiar with the rules of verse composition than those who teach them.

What was once second nature to English poets—scanning and even composing Latin verse—has thus become largely a historical curiosity. And what once would have seemed a reasonable thing to do—writing one's native verse according to the rules learned in

Latin class—now seems quaint and bizarre. Most literary historians and poetry instructors know how important classical education was to English poets but often dismiss it by characterizing the few eccentric attempts to impose these schoolboy rules of Latin versification on English as failures: too bad Philip Sidney and Thomas Campion attempted to write in quantitative verse; they should have known better. Hearing such things, and recalling the gobbledegook they have been taught in the past, intelligent students can only conclude that versification is a subject not worth knowing.

| The first part of my discussion deals with quantitative Latin verse, a verse form in which nearly all English poets from the sixteenth to the twentieth century were trained. Other verse systems I discuss are the classical French syllabic systems and early Germanic accentual verse as it was understood by modern scholars of this literature. I have chosen these examples not because they represent versification in general or even European versification. Latin, French, and Old English exemplify, rather, what are often described as three basic forms of versification in the West: quantitative verse, syllabic or isosyllabic verse, and accentual verse. Other languages might serve just as well, and perhaps better. But I am less familiar with them. To these three, I have added a chapter on what could be called the verse of libretti—that is, verse entirely controlled by extra-verbal music. As for English verse, despite the assurances of some introductory guides to English meter, there is no single system that reasonably applies to the English tradition generally, nor is one proposed here; I thus deal only with select cases in chapter 6.

Rules of Latin and French versification changed as the language changed. What I provide here are particular slices of these histories. I ignore the early history of Latin verse that shaped Roman poets (i.e., early Saturnian verse) as well as the transformation of Latin in the Middle Ages and describe the far more stable system of Latin versification as taught in schools. For French, I concentrate on a few specific issues (e.g., the caesura) on which much of the development of French verse was felt to depend. Descriptions of early Germanic verse are changing; I focus here on the one that has provided the basic vocabulary for verse types to most students in the twentieth century. Finally, I use the self-evident differences between classical composers such as Giulio Caccini and Richard Wagner and the blues artist Robert Johnson to sketch the lurking problem of musical forms in verse. Music was at the base of much of what is now printed as verse; and it is music to which the language of much of our poetics still inadvertently alludes, with terms such as *musicality, tone,* and *rhythm.*

I have made no attempt at a universal terminology or a new self-consistent system of notation to describe these various systems. The terminology used to describe classical verse works reasonably well to describe classical verse, and the somewhat different language developed in the Middle Ages to describe French verse has proven to be useful for that purpose even through the twentieth century. I will thus use the simplest forms of these conventional languages of verse description as long as they are not inaccurate or positively misleading. I will avoid if possible the most obvious sources of ambiguity, and, when those ambiguities cannot be avoided, explain at least why they exist. When the conventional language fails, I will use the most common language I can.

Classical verse was not composed on the same principles as modern verse. To say that English blank verse is unrhymed iambic pentameter is misleading and in my opinion flat out wrong, and to imply that English verse can be analyzed coherently in such terminology borders on mystification. Our hypothetically attentive and intelligent students are told to analyze Shakespeare according to whatever rules of iambic pentameter might be drawn up on the board; having forgotten, perhaps, that versification is not worth knowing, they will now conclude, reasonably enough, that such matters are simply beyond human comprehension. But they're not. It's just that the anatomical description of an elephant is not necessarily the best language to use in describing, say, a house fire or an internal combustion engine.

Resources

There are many guides to foreign versification designed for English students, and a growing number of these—some useful, some dated, and many rapidly changing—have appeared on the internet. Among the more notable printed guides are Lewis Turco, *The Book of Forms: A Handbook of Poetics* (2000); John Hollander, *Rhyme's Reason: A Guide to English Verse* (1981); and the anthology by William K. Wimsatt, *Versification: Major Language Types, Sixteen Essays* (1971). These are good introductions, but most omit much of the basic and essential prosodic detail, detail that is essential for their readers to have any idea of what their examples mean. Hollander's manual is an exercise in poetic virtuosity, and much of it is composed in the meters that are being described. But without knowing the precise details of those meters, a reader is lost. You can only understand this manual if you are able to write it; reading it is unfortunately not enough.

Serious and detailed presentations of Latin, French, or German verse systems are generally found only in language instruction manuals and thus are not easily accessible for most students in classes in English literature. One learns the principles of Latin hexameter as a third-year Latin student, French Alexandrines as an advanced French student. These manuals tend not to condescend to their readers, and few make detailed information accessible to anyone who does not already have a fairly good grasp of it. One can extract most of what I say about Latin verse in such books as *Introduction to Latin Meter* by D. S. Raven (1965) or *The Meters of Greek and Latin Poetry* by James W. Halporn, Martin Ostwald, and Thomas Rosenmeyer (1963; rev. 1980). Also useful are the sections on meter in once-standard grammar books, such as Allen and Greenough's *Latin Grammar for Schools and Colleges,* a text that has been through over a century of editions and revisions and is now available online. Editions of classical poets designed for schools also contain valuable sections on meter. Yet, most material is presented as reference (that is, readers apparently know the basic principles of Horace's verse and need only to brush up on the fine points of, say, the scansion of a Fifth Asclepiad). Even to an intermediate Latin student, such guides are intimidating, and advanced Latinists will often struggle with many of the details; to non-Latinists, they are nearly impenetrable. In addition, modern student editions of standard Latin texts rarely mark naturally long vowels, and many versification manuals omit them as well, despite the fact that these details are essential to the meter of Latin; this may or may not be a morally and pedagogically sound way to teach language, but it makes versification far more difficult for all but fluent Latinists.

For French, specific and detailed rules of prosody and versification have been articulated and debated by critics and poets for centuries, and there are, fortunately, many excellent discussions available in English; L. E. Kastner's *A History of French Versification* (1903) is itself the basis for standard guides to French versification now published in French, in particular, W. Th. Elwert, *Traité de versification française des origines à nos jours* (1965) (originally in German, now a basic manual in French). The situation with early Germanic verse is a bit better. The majority of those who have studied Old English and bought books on this subject are introductory students, and serious discussion of verse, therefore, often appears in introductory handbooks. The section on meter in the revision of *Bright's Old English Grammar and Reader* (1972) is no less accessible to the first-year student than to the advanced one. Yet, like similar studies in classics, these discussions tend to be ancillary and for students primarily interested in the languages themselves; there are, as far as I know, no studies that present this material in a form that is both accessible to intelligent students who have not been trained in these languages and detailed enough to be interesting to such students.

An assumption made in many general discussions of versification, including those mentioned above, is that to understand verse is to understand poetry; this assumption is particularly noticeable in works from the 1960s and 1970s such as Paul Fussell's *Poetic Meter and Poetic Form* (1965; rev. ed. New York, 1979), and in the articles and subjects dealt with in the various editions of the *Princeton Encyclopedia of Poetry and Poetics,* ed. Alex J. Preminger (1962; new edition, 1993). It is basic to the way literature was taught to most of us: form is meaning. Scholarly books and monographs that discuss the versification practices of particular authors tend to share this assumption; Dante's hendecasyllable, if worthy of discussion, must partake somehow of that grander thing, Dante's poetics. But the collapsing of these various levels of poetic phenomena obscures all of them. Versification is one thing; style is something else. And poetry, whatever that is, may well be something else again. There are lines from the *Aeneid* whose versification is quite obvious, yet their meaning eludes me; similarly, there are lines from Wallace Stevens I understand completely, yet I have no idea what their metrical basis might be.

The organization of some of my chapters differs in one important way from that of standard manuals. I am concerned here less with coverage, that is, a systematic synopsis of each verse type, than with accessibility. I spend more time on what is easily understood than on what is not; for Latin, I begin with dactylic hexameter, not because this form is basic in a theoretical or historical sense, but because it was the form learned first by and most familiar to centuries of Latin schoolchildren. Those who are willing to understand this form but lose heart when it comes to the intricacies of dramatic verse can gloss over the more difficult forms in later sections or ignore them entirely, as students and teachers alike have done for centuries. For French verse, I concentrate on the classical Alexandrine because this was the form subject to the most debate in the history of French poetics. The principles behind these forms (or more precisely, the principles thought to be behind them) are not overly controversial nor are they difficult to learn. This guide should provide enough material to enable readers to scan most common Latin verse types, to distinguish classical French verse from its late nineteenth-century variants, to scan a few lines from *Beowulf,* and, in this last case, to understand why once-standard scansion has been critiqued. It should also indicate how such systems operate or could operate in particular English poems. Ideally, this guide will demystify some of the discussions on verse to which students of English literature have been subjected and enable them to see when the obscurity of these discussions has sources other than the impenetrability of the subject.

Chapter One

Basic Principles

A. Syllable and Line

Verse is the organization of words according to units represented graphically and typographically as *lines*. Such lines are potentially repeatable. The most basic linguistic unit that defines and constitutes these lines is the *syllable*. Although we all know, more or less, what a syllable is, a syllable is difficult to define linguistically; and what might be called a syllable in speech or in the history of a language is not the same as what is considered a syllable in verse. The prosodic value of a syllable—that is, the way a linguistic syllable is treated in verse—is based on, but not necessarily the same as, the linguistic value or phonetic reality of that syllable.

A.1. Syllables are treated differently in different verse systems. They may be undifferentiated, that is, the prosodic value of all syllables is the same, or they may be distinguished, either by accent (stressed vs. unstressed) or by quantity (long vs. short). The following are basic verse types categorized by syllable treatment:

> *quantitative:* a line consists of a given pattern of long and short syllables

isosyllabic: a line consists of a given number of syllables

accentual: a line consists of a given pattern of stressed and unstressed syllables

A.1.1. The above terms are conventionally used to describe historical European verse; Latin is usefully described as quantitative verse,
French as isosyllabic, early Germanic verse as accentual (the basis for
the organization of chapters 2–4 below). In the strictest sense, these
descriptions are not accurate, since both French and Latin verse
have supplemental rules of accent, and early Germanic verse incorporates rules of syllable count and quantity. Furthermore, the three
categories may privilege English verse, which is sometimes described
as "accentual-syllabic" (so Hollander, *Rhyme's Reason*; and Fussell, *Poetic Meter and Poetic Form*; see introduction above, "Resources"). But
such a category may be illusory. The principles of English verse generally should be described as variable, or as simply "unknown."

A.1.2. Pure forms of quantitative, isosyllabic, and accentual verse
types are certainly possible, even though historical forms (Latin,
French, and early Germanic) are less pure than often described.
There is nothing to prevent a poet from defining rules of composition that would involve accent only; and strictly isosyllabic forms
exist in the experimental verse of Robert Bridges and Marianne
Moore (see chap. 6, B.2). What appear to be nearly pure forms of
syllabic verse may also be found in verse composed for music, although such verse is controlled by extralinguistic factors (see chap. 6,
D on the verse of John Donne).

A.2. Verse Types and Notation

Because the bases for historical verse differ, no single system of notation can adequately describe all verse, and I have tried to use the simplest, most self-explanatory system in my descriptions below. For isosyllabic and syllabic verse, I simply use an x to mark a syllable; I note
a required accent with an uppercase X. I use roughly the same notation for early Germanic verse forms: X and x distinguish accented
from unaccented syllables or their equivalent. For quantitative verse,
I mark syllables as long and short (_ and ˘; a syllable position that

can be occupied by either a long or a short is marked x). There are numerous ways of describing what is called accentual-syllabic verse: the system of notation associated with the influential work of linguists Morris Halle and Samuel Jay Keyser distinguishes strong and weak syllables as S W. Thus, what is commonly described as iambic pentameter in their system would be WSWSWSWSWS or even 5(WS). This might also be written x ´ x ´ x ´ x ´ x ´ or, as here, x X x X x X x X x X; an accented lowercase x might be used for my uppercase X, but such choices are often dictated less by theory than by what is available on a computer font. Single and double vertical lines are generally used to mark foot breaks and caesurae respectively, and I follow those conventions below. I use the same notation both to describe abstract, idealized line patterns and to analyze particular lines. Occasionally some modification is necessary, and particular details of notation will be discussed as the need arises.

A.3. Basic Units of the Line: Foot, Metron, and Colon

A.3.1. The syllables that form a line may be organized into larger units. The unit most familiar to English readers is the *foot,* which for some verse types is considered the minimal unit of composition. Types of feet have names based on Greek meter: the iamb (x X or x ´ in accentual verse, ⏑ — in quantitative verse), the dactyl (X x x in accentual verse, — ⏑ ⏑ in quantitative verse), etc. The ten-syllable line represented above in section A.2 could be described as five repeating units of an iambic foot: x X | x X | x X | x X | x X. Another way of saying the same thing is iambic pentameter. The foot is not a basic unit of composition in the way that a line is basic; and there are many verse types, including French verse generally, that cannot be analyzed in terms of feet.

A.3.2. Metron and Colon

In other verse types, the minimal unit of composition is the *metron* (pl. *metra*). Greek iambic trimeter is considered three four-syllable units (x — ⏑ —) of metra rather than six two-syllable iambic units (⏑ —) of feet. A unit longer than the metron is the *colon* (pl. *cola*). In some verse, the colon is a unit less than a line in length (a half-line, or the *hemiepes* in an elegiac couplet; see chap. 2, D.2). In other verse, the colon is the line itself (the *glyconic,* chap. 2, B.1.5). The study of cola is known as *colometry*. In practice, however, colometry almost always refers to the construction and representation of the lines themselves, not necessarily the cola.

B. Line Combinations: The Stanza

Combinations of lines are generally named after the number of lines per unit: *distich* or *couplet* (two lines), *tercet* (three lines), *quatrain* (four lines). These units can be defined either by rhyme scheme or by syntax. A fourteen-line Shakespearean sonnet thus can be analyzed as three quatrains followed by a rhyming couplet; each quatrain along with the concluding couplet has independent rhyming elements and each generally consists of a complete and autonomous syntactic unit. A larger unit of composition is the stanza: any formal pattern of lines that is potentially repeatable. In most poems, the stanza is repeated, although there are exceptions (see chap. 2, H on dramatic *cantica* and chap. 5, B.2.2 on the English ode). A stanza may or may not contain units such as the couplet or quatrain. Comparing stanzas in any poem will likely indicate the principles involved in their production.

B.1. Units such as couplets and quatrains, as well as stanza units, are traditionally indicated visually in both manuscripts and printed books, although the conventions for doing so are far from universal. In medieval manuscripts, rhymes are sometimes joined by marginal brackets. In printed books, stanzas are represented typographically, usually by a line space separating them.

B.2. Many stanza types are traditional. And for these (the French "fixed forms," for example), basic principles are easily enough expressed in a table indicating line length and rhyme scheme. But for many other common but less traditional stanza types, the rules underlying verse structure are not so easily systematized, as in verse associated with musical compositions. Poets may compose stanzas according to any rules—accentual, syllabic, or even arbitrary rules unique to a poem—and they may overlay a pattern of line structures with a rhyme structure that can either support it or act as counterpoint. There is no theoretical limit to the length and complexity of a stanza. In English, examples of very complex forms are found in the odes of the seventeenth and eighteenth centuries (see chap. 5, B.2).

C. Stylistic Elements

Elements that are basic to the metrical structure of a verse should be distinguished from elements that are ornamental or aesthetic. While the latter stylistic elements are certainly crucial to what could be called the art of a verse, they are not foundational to the verse. There are, unfortunately, no absolute rules to distinguish between basic and stylistic elements. And certain verse features that are basic elements of versification in one system might be ornamental in another. In Greek hexameter, word accent is at best ornamental; Latin hexameter, however, has strict rules regarding the metrical use of this accent and implied rules regarding its aesthetic use. In some early Germanic verse, rules of alliteration are fundamental to the verse; thus the alliteration on the initial *m-* in the Old English line "metudes miltse, þēah þe hē mōdcearig," is basic; without it, the line would be unmetrical. In modern English verse, alliteration is a purely ornamental matter, and a line is metrical regardless of whether it alliterates. Thus in Shakespeare's *Love's Labour's Lost*:

> Why? all delights are vaine, and that most vaine
> Which with paine purchas'd, doth inherit paine,
> As painefully to poare upon a Booke
> To seeke the light of truth, while truth the while . . .
> (act 1, sc. 1)

Here, the alliteration "paine purchas'd" is purely ornamental, as are such other potentially structural features as the rhyming "vaine . . . vaine . . . delights . . . light . . . ," etc. Because the function of such elements varies in different verse systems, general definitions of basic and stylistic elements can be misleading.

C.1. Complicating this distinction is the fact that stylistic elements, even when not part of the fundamental structure of a verse line, can become so conventional that they begin to partake of the basic character of a verse. A line of an English heroic couplet in the eighteenth

century will probably have a word break after the fourth or fifth syllable, even though a line that does not show such a break is not necessarily unmetrical (see chap. 6, B):

> 'Tis hard to say, if greater Want of Skill
> Appear in Writing, or in Judging ill . . .
>   (Alexander Pope, *Essay on Criticism*)

Early blues artists such as Son House and Robert Johnson "dropped"
beats so regularly that the strict rhythmic conventions followed by
some later blues artists seem almost unnatural (see chap. 5, D).

D. Levels of Description

What we call verse and its patterns can exist on a number of levels.
Verse, for example, could be considered a predetermined abstract
pattern that poets self-consciously try to produce; it could be the actual verbal patterns that are produced on paper, or the somewhat
different abstract patterns that a reader expects. In addition, verse
could encompass the patterns implied by particular readings and
performances, or the abstract classifications that apply to them. And
what to a literary critic or student of metrics would be a perfectly coherent account of one of these levels might be baffling to the poets
themselves. A satisfactory description of verse on one level is not necessarily a satisfactory account of verse on any other level.

In most cases, the differences between the various levels are not
overly troublesome, and most of the ambiguities can be negotiated.
When we give rules for some basic verse types (say, Latin hexameter),
those rules serve as tools of analysis. When we can speak of them as
part of the poet's basic rules of composition, we are speaking metaphorically and make no claims as to what was going on in any particular poet's head. We suspect that Latin poets, being fluent in Latin
as we are not, had something other than our rules in mind. In addition, real readers, even the individual authors of certain poems, could
and do perform the same poem in different ways. In a sense, the individual written poem is itself a performance of the verse system it
implies.

Thus the crassest answers that the language of classical verse
description might give to questions concerning these levels are the

following: But what is going on in a poet's head? *We don't know.* But what about how Lawrence Olivier (or my friend Fred) reads that line? *We don't care.* A more reasoned but no more satisfying or accurate response might be: versification is the study and classification of the abstract forms implied by real verses; it is not the study of poetry as an art and it is not the study of performances of particular poems. But even that answer might fail in certain contexts, since different genres define the significance of these levels in different ways: Would we so easily ignore the performance conventions of the early blues artists mentioned above? Is not the essence of the form expressed in the very rhythmic and intonational irregularities we hear?

E. English Verse

Missing here is the chapter that English readers might expect to be basic, and that is a systematic chapter on the principles of English versification. I have confined my discussion of English verse to the specific cases in chapter 6 and the brief comments on the teaching of English in my conclusion. There simply are no universal rules of English verse production; or at least, in my study of English verse from early medieval to modern verse, I haven't been able to find them. Students have known this for as long as I have been in and around schools, perplexed as they rightly have been over bizarre explanations that require "To BE or NOT to BE that IS . . . ," or explanations that can't seem to get us past line 1 of the *Canterbury Tales*: is it "When THAT ApRILLe WITH . . . ," or is it perhaps "WHANN-uh that A-PRILL-uh . . ."? But the incomprehensibility of English versification should not lead students to believe in the incomprehensibility of all versification. I hope the presentation of these systems, often borrowed and imitated by English poets, will at least give the student of this tradition a place to start.

Quantitative Verse

Classical Latin

Classical Greek and Latin verse is quantitative, that is, it is dominated by and organized according to distinctions between long and short syllables. A Latin dactylic hexameter is a line of six dactyls or their equivalent. Analyzed according to feet, it can be represented in the following scheme, whereby each foot consists of a long syllable followed by two short syllables (the symbol > is conventionally used to indicate a terminal syllable that can be either long or short):

$$\_ \smile \smile \mid \_ \smile \smile \mid \_ \smile \smile \mid \_ \smile \smile \mid \_ \smile \smile \mid \_ >$$

A common form of the hendecasyllable (an eleven-syllable line) might be represented as follows (the double vertical line represents a conventional word break):

$$\_ \_ \smile \_ \_ \parallel \_ \smile \smile \_ \smile >$$

The word we use to describe such analysis is *scansion*.

This chapter begins with the most common verse types and moves through more complex forms. With the detail provided here, even non-Latinists should be able to scan and imitate the epic forms (sec. D) and many of the lyric forms (sec. E). Further examples of verse types are given in the appendix. The scansion of iambic and trochaic forms, especially their dramatic varieties, poses far more difficulties (secs. F and G); my discussion of these forms is thus less detailed, since it would be unreasonable if not cruel to expect anyone other than a skilled Latinist to be able to scan, say, an extended passage from Terence.

A. Basic Elements
A.1. Rules for Determining Syllable Length
Syllables in Latin verse are analyzed as long or short. A syllable is considered long in the following cases:

   a) *The syllable contains a naturally long vowel.*

Note: Latin vowels are distinguished linguistically as long or short. These differences would be obvious to native speakers and vowel length is marked in modern dictionaries. Some naturally long vowels can be determined by rule: e.g., final *-o* or *-i* are nearly always long. Vowel length is not represented graphically in written or printed Latin (in Greek, the difference between, say, long and short *-o-* is represented as a difference between an omicron and an omega). For non-Latinists, it is convenient to find texts where editors have marked naturally long vowels. Introductory Latin books generally do this, as do many student texts printed in the early twentieth century; most standard editions, however, do not, even those designed for students.

   b) *The syllable contains a diphthong, that is, a monosyllabic vowel sound expressed graphically as two vowels.* Examples: *-oi-* and *-ae* in the two-syllable word *Troiae.*

Note: Most double vowel combinations in Latin are not diphthongs. A *u* following *q-* is not a true vowel but an indication of the quality of the consonant. Thus "quis" does not contain a diphthong. In "quae" the diphthong is *ae*. Both words are monosyllables. The same is true of other words such as *cui*. An apparent double vowel (*-ii-*) is two syllables, not a diphthong. The rule is sometimes blurred in that some two-syllable vowel combinations can be scanned as one syllable: děĭndě (trisyllabic) becomes děindě (disyllabic). This is called *synizesis.*

c) *In a line of verse the syllable is followed by two or more consonants.* Thus, the first syllable of *arma* is long. In the phrase *Ītaliam fatō, Ītaliam* is a four-syllable word that consists linguistically of one long syllable (the initial *I* is long by nature) followed by three short syllables: _ ◡ ◡ ◡. But in the metrical context above, *Ītaliam* is scanned _ ◡ ◡ _, since the last vowel (*-a-*) is followed by two consonants.

Note: In some descriptions of Latin verse, this rule is expressed in terms of open and closed syllables. A syllable is open if it ends in a vowel, closed if it ends in a consonant; syllable division within a word places an internal consonant with the preceding vowel. A closed syllable is considered long metrically if it is followed by a syllable beginning with a consonant. It is considered short if it is followed by a syllable beginning with a vowel. I do not see the advantage of this explanation over the mechanical one above, which does not require defining the precise elements in each syllable.

c.1) The consonants *x* and *z* are considered double consonants.

c.2) A special case of double consonants concerns the combination of a *mute* (or "stop") followed by a *liquid*. In Greek, the rule includes a mute followed by nasals *m* and *n*, but in Latin, *m* and *n* do not occur naturally in these combinations. Linguistically, the mutes can be analyzed as three sets: unvoiced (*p, t, k*); voiced (*b, d, g*); aspirate (*f, th, h*) (*k* and *h* do not occur as mutes in Latin). Liquids are *l, r.* A syllable containing a naturally short vowel followed by the consonant combination of a mute and a liquid can be metrically long or metrically short. This rule applies only when the combination of the mute and liquid occurs in the same syllable: for example, the initial *fr-* in *frāter.* In a word such as *oblino,* composed of the separate elements *ob-* plus *-lino,* the two consonants are part of different syllables, and the syllable *ob-* would be considered long.

d) *Exceptions.* There are certain cases where the above rules for determining syllable length are not strictly applied. The most important involves what is known as *brevis brevians.* This rule is variously stated, but in its simplest form, a long syllable can be counted short if it is followed or preceded by a short syllable that itself has the "word accent," or stress (see sec. B.3.1 below). Brevis brevians commonly involves disyllabic words: the word *bŏnīs* can be scanned as two shorts even when followed by a consonant combination. Fortunately for non-Latinists, whose notion of naturally long vowels may be hazy and flexible to begin with, this rule will not prove troublesome.

A.2. Elision and Hiatus

A.2.1. Elision

When a word ending in a vowel is followed by a word beginning with a vowel, the final vowel of the first word is *elided,* that is, it is dropped and not counted in the scansion of a line, and its quantity (long or short) is disregarded. In the phrase *ille ego,* the final *-e* of *ille* is dropped, and the entire phrase scanned _ ◡ ◡. In addition, a word ending in a vowel plus *-m* is treated as a word ending in a vowel; that is, the *-um* will be elided if it is followed by a word beginning with a vowel. In the phrase *multum ille, -um* is effectively dropped, and the phrase scanned _ _ ◡. For all practical purposes, the letter *h* is not considered (metrically) as a letter at all. Thus when a word ending in a vowel is followed by a word beginning with an *h* plus a vowel, the vowel of the first word is elided. The same rule applies when a word ending in vowel plus *-m* is followed by a word beginning with *h* plus a vowel: the final syllable of the first word is also elided. Certain common monosyllabic words are not elided, for example, *dō* (I give), *spem* (hope [accusative case]), *quī* (they).

A.2.2. Hiatus

Hiatus is most simply seen as an exception to the general rule of elision. It refers to specific cases where normal elision does not occur. Some cases are stylistic: Vergil, for example, might treat the initial *h* as a consonant in some words of Greek origin. Other cases of hiatus are metrical: in certain positions of the line, the implied break might be so prominent as to prevent elision.

A.3. Basic Substitutions

Rules of substitution are specific to verse type. In some verse types, substitution is based on quantity: two shorts are the metrical equivalent of one long. Thus in dactylic hexameter, a dactyl can be replaced by a spondee: _ ◡ ◡ is essentially equivalent metrically to _ _. In lyric verse, substitutions often involve single syllables: certain line positions can be occupied by either one short or one long syllable. Thus, the initial two syllables of an Aeolic line can be either long or short. Such a syllable is called *anceps;* in scansion it is generally marked with an x. Dramatic verse involves both types of substitutions (i.e., by quantity and by syllable length); in certain foot positions in a Latin iambic senarius (sec. B.1.4 below), the iamb (◡ _) can be replaced by a dactyl (_ ◡ ◡; long for the short in the first position, two shorts for the long in the second), a spondee (_ _; long for the short in the first position), or even ◡ ◡ ◡ ◡ (long for the short in the first position, and resolution of both longs as two shorts).[1]

A.4. The rules detailed in sections A.1–A.3 are sufficient to scan most common Latin lines: for example, the opening line of Vergil's *Aeneid*:

arma virumque canō, Troiae quī prīmus ab ōrīs.

The naturally long vowels and diphthongs identify one set of long syllables:

‒   ‒   ‒   ‒   ‒   ‒ ‒

arma virumque canō, Troi-ae quī prīmus ab ōrīs

To these can be added syllables that are "long by position," that is, syllables that contain a vowel followed by two consonants:

‒   ‒

*ar*ma vi*rum*que . . .

Since each foot must contain either a dactyl (_ ◡ ◡) or a spondee (_ _), a little inspection and experimentation will show that there is

---

1. There are several ways of representing such substitutions, and some schemes simply list the potential substitutions singly: ◡ _ / ◡ ◡ ◡ / _ _ / _ ◡ ◡ / etc. Although an anceps syllable is written x, there is little practical difference between x, _ / ◡, and other ways of indicating this. Final syllables that are similarly long or short are conventionally represented with the symbol >.

only one way to fit six such feet into the above pattern. We can thus scan the line as follows; the break between feet is noted as a single vertical line (|):

$$\_\ \ \smile\ \smile\ |\_\ \ \smile\ \ \ \smile\ |\_\ \_\ |\_\ \ \_\ |\_\ \ \smile\ \ \smile\ |\_ >$$
arma virumque canō, Troiae quī prīmus ab ōrīs.

The following line from Horace is scanned as a hendecasyllable (see sec. E.1 below); there is nothing that corresponds to a foot break, although Horace in this form conventionally has a word break following syllable 5, which some scholars represent with a single or double vertical line.

$$\_\ \ \smile\ \ \_\ \_\ \_\ \ \ \smile\ \ \ \smile\ \_\ \smile\ \ \ \_\ \ \smile$$
Integer vītae scelerisque pūrus

B. Elements of the Line: Foot and Metron, Caesura and Diaeresis, Word Accent and Verse Accent

B.1. Foot and Metron

Some Latin verse is organized by the foot (a minimal metrical unit); other verse is organized by larger metrical units, the metron or the colon, many of which cannot be usefully analyzed in feet. The types of feet frequently invoked in discussions of verse in English are *iamb, trochee, spondee, dactyl,* and *anapest.*

B.1.1. Disyllabic Feet:

iamb	$\smile\ \_$
trochee	$\_\ \smile$
spondee	$\_\ \_$
pyrrhic	$\smile\ \smile$

B.1.2. Trisyllabic Feet:

dactyl	$\_\ \smile\ \smile$
anapest	$\smile\ \smile\ \_$

Less common trisyllabic feet are the following:

cretic   — ˘ —
bacchiac   ˘ _ _
amphibrach   _ _ ˘
molossus   _ _ _
tribrach   ˘ ˘ ˘

Other forms of trisyllabic feet include the *palimbacchiac:* _ _ ˘ (a "backward bacchiac"). It is doubtful whether the *molossus* and *tribrach* should be considered true feet, since they clearly could not be the basic units of a verse, and they are rarely used in descriptions of basic verse patterns; they occur (as does the disyllabic spondee) as possible substitutions for other feet in dramatic verse (sec. F.2 below).

B.1.3. Four-Syllable Feet:

choriamb   _ ˘ ˘ _
ionic   ˘ ˘ _ _

The *choriamb* is the most common of these; a form such as the *proceleusmatic* (˘ ˘ ˘ ˘) occurs as a possible substitution in some verse feet (e.g., in some iambic verse), but it is not a basic unit of any verse type.

B.1.4. The Metron
Some verse lines are formed by larger units of feet, and in some cases it is useful to speak of this unit as a *metron* (pl. *metra*). Thus, in Greek, an iambic trimeter is conventionally analyzed as three groups of metra, each metron composed of two iambic feet. The equivalent meter in Latin is the iambic senarius (a line of six metrical feet; see sec. F.2.1 below). The reason for this difference has to do with the Greek and Latin rules regarding each unit. In Greek, the rules of substitution that apply to feet 1, 3, and 5 are different from those that apply to 2, 4, and 6, but the rules that apply to each of the three four-syllable units are essentially the same. In Latin, the same rules of substitution apply to each foot.

B.1.5. Units longer than the foot or metron are sometimes known as *cola* (sing. *colon*). Among the commonly named cola is the *glyconic,* characterized by an internal choriamb (_ ◡ ◡ _): x x _ ◡ ◡ _ ◡ _. Without the final long syllable, the colon is a *pherecratean* (x x _ ◡ ◡ _ >); with the addition of a final syllable, it is a *hipponactean* (x x _ ◡ ◡ _ ◡ _ >). Some scholars of metrics analyze these lines as consisting of four feet; others describe them as containing a moveable internal dactyl. But lines that do not consist of repeating units of feet or metra are most easily analyzed by considering the line itself (the colon) as the basic unit.

B.2. Caesura and Diaeresis
B.2.1. Caesura

There are two meanings of the word *caesura*. The general sense applicable particularly to French verse is a prominent syntactic break in a line (see chap. 3, C). While this can apply to some Latin verse, the technical sense relevant to most Latin verse is a word break that occurs within a verse foot, that is, a word break that does not correspond with a foot break. When discussing Latin verse, I will confine the word to this meaning. Most dactylic hexameters have a caesura in the third foot, marked here with a double vertical line:

$$ \_ \quad ◡ \quad ◡ \mid \_ \quad ◡ \quad ◡ \mid \_ \parallel \_ \mid \_ $$

Arma virumque canō || Troiae

In such verse, the word break does not correspond to the foot break in the third foot. Some lyric forms do not permit word breaks in certain positions, and this may be indicated in some systems of scansion by joining the syllable marks _ ◡ ◡ (_◡ ◡), or by an inverted ◡ (⌢◡ ◡). Such a position is known as a *bridge*.

B.2.2. Diaeresis

A *diaeresis* is the coincidence of a foot break and a word break. In some verse, the placement becomes so conventional that it is given a name; a word break occurring between the fourth and fifth feet of a dactylic hexameter, for example, is the *bucolic diaeresis* (see sec. D.1.4 below). An example is the opening line of Vergil's *Eclogues*:

$$ \_ ◡ ◡ \mid \_ \quad ◡ ◡ \mid \_ \quad ◡ ◡ \mid \_ \quad \_ \parallel \_ \quad ◡ \quad ◡ \mid \_ > $$

Tītyre, tū patulae recubāns sub tegmine fāgī

B.3. Additional Elements of Line Structure

B.3.1. Word Accent vs. Verse Accent

Linguistically, every Latin word has a *word accent* (a stress). This accent can occur on either a long or a short syllable.[2] The word accent, also called a phonetic accent or linguistic accent, is different from the *verse accent* (or *ictus*). The verse accent is simply the long syllable in the foot (the second syllable of an iambic, the first of a trochee). Verse accent has nothing to do with the linguistic stress (word accent) of the word itself. Word accent is disregarded in Greek verse; in Latin verse, it is generally a secondary matter, although certain verse types have rules or conventions that involve this accent.

B.3.2. Arsis and Thesis

In Latin, the *arsis* is generally (but not always!) considered the heavy or long element of a verse foot; the *thesis* is the unstressed element; for an iamb ($\smile$ $\_$), the arsis in the Latin sense is the second syllable; the thesis the first. These terms are ambiguous, since they can be used in exactly the opposite sense of the one defined here. Latin verse can be easily described without them.[3]

---

2. In Latin, the placement of word accent is regular and follows specific rules. In disyllabic words, the accent is on the first syllable. In multisyllabic words, when the next to last syllable is long, that syllable contains the word accent. When the next to last syllable is short, the preceding syllable contains the accent.

3. The terms unfortunately are not avoided in standard discussions of classical verse. In classical Greek, "arsis" referred to the raising of a real foot in marching; "thesis" referred to the placing of the foot down on the ground. Thus the thesis in Greek verse was the "beat" (in music, the downbeat—the OOM, in OOM pa pa) and the same as the verse accent. In a dactyl, the thesis was the first long, the arsis the remaining shorts. In Latin, this terminology was reversed: the "arsis" became the implied "raising" of the voice in stress, and thus, the arsis of the dactyl in Latin verse was described as the initial long (the verse accent), and the thesis the rest of the verse. Nineteenth-century scholars of early Germanic verse imposed the Latin misuse of these terms onto Germanic verse, although its underlying system had nothing to do with either Greek or Latin. Curiously, some early twentieth-century Greek grammar books adopted the Latin use as well, while some of the most important Latin grammar books returned to the Greek form. Useful as these terms might be, only the person using them can be certain of their intended meaning.

B.4. English Imitations and Versions

There are many ways of imitating Latin verse or verse forms in English. To do so requires defining the English equivalent of the linguistic distinction between long and short syllables. Most English writers represent this in English as a difference between stressed and unstressed syllables; that is, the quantitative distinction (long vs. short) is transformed into one involving stress (stressed vs. unstressed). Thus the word *living* in English would be scanned as a two-syllable word with a stress on the first syllable: X x, that is, as a trochee. But there have been attempts to apply rules of quantity directly to English verse. The word *living* would be scanned differently under these rules: if one disregards the linguistic stress, the word can be scanned as a short syllable (*liv-*) followed by a long one (*-ing*, long due to the consonant combination in *-ng*). Quantitatively, the word *liv-ing* can thus be scanned ⌣ —, that is, as an iamb.[4] See chapter 5 for examples from Renaissance writers.

C. Basic Line Types

C.1. Basic line types based on feet include such forms as (a) *dactylic hexameter:* a line consists of dactyls or their equivalent organized in six feet; (b) *iambic senarius:* a line consists of iambs organized in six feet; (c) *trochaic septenarius:* a line consists of seven trochaic feet.

C.1.1. Trochaic and iambic line types (sec. F) are often described as lacking the final syllable and thus *catalectic;* lines described as lacking the initial syllable of the first foot are called "headless" or *acephalic.* Thus a *catalectic trochaic septenarius* consists of seven feet of trochees, lacking the final short syllable.

C.2. Meters can also be based on metra (the Greek equivalent of the Latin iambic senarius is called a *trimeter:* three metra, each consisting

---

4. A useful exercise for English students for understanding the implications of quantitative meter is to begin with a well known and heavily accented line such as a limerick: "There wás a young lády of Róme," scanned x X x x X x x X. This pattern can then be reproduced using quantitative rules (⌣ — — ⌣ ⌣ — ⌣ ⌣ —): "a young woman of Tripoli." Here, long syllables are those with a vowel followed by two or more consonants (*young* and *of* are scanned long), and the linguistic accent is disregarded (*woman* is thus scanned as two shorts).

of the equivalent of two iambic feet). Others are based on larger units of the colon or the line itself (see secs. B.1.4 and B.1.5 above). Irregular *cantica* (sec. H) would be analyzed by cola as would the Aeolic verse described below (sec. E).

C.2.1. The hendecasyllable is an eleven-syllable line, whose most common form in Latin is associated with Catullus: _ x _ ◡ ◡ _ ◡ _ ◡ _ ◡; the form in Greek is associated with Sappho: _ ◡ _ x _ ◡ ◡ _ ◡ _ _. Both forms are occasionally analyzed in feet (for example, the Catullus hendecasyllable might be analyzed as a trochee, a dactyl, and three trochees), and they can also, with difficulty, be seen as forms of the eight-syllable glyconic (see sec. B.1.5 above). But little is gained by such gymnastics; it's easier simply to write the scansion out.

D. Epic Types
D.1. Dactylic Hexameter
We have used this line type to illustrate many of the principles of Latin versification. A basic description of the line in terms of feet is as follows:

$$\_ \, ◡ \, ◡ \mid \_ \, ◡ \, ◡ \mid \_ \, ◡ \, ◡ \mid \_ \, ◡ \, ◡ \mid \_ \, ◡ \, ◡ \mid \_ >$$

In English, the dactylic hexameter is often written in an accentual form, as in Longfellow's *Evangeline*: "This is the forest primeval, the murmuring pines in the hemlock."

D.1.1. A spondee can be used in place of a dactyl in any of the first four feet. In Latin, such a substitution in the fifth foot is so rare as to be considered impermissible.

D.1.2. Word accent in a Latin hexameter invariably coincides with verse accent in the fifth and sixth feet. In Greek verse, there are no rules regarding word accent, and spondees are admitted in the fifth foot.

D.1.3. Caesura
A caesura (in the strict sense) generally occurs in the third foot of a dactylic hexameter. And classical Latin verse generally avoids the co-

incidence of word break and foot break (diaeresis) in the first part of the line.

arma virumque canō || Troiae quī prīmus ab ōrīs

Although the caesura appears to be an ornamental matter, it is nearly essential to the classical form of the dactylic hexameter. And while a line with word breaks corresponding to foot breaks between feet 2, 3, and 4 might not be considered unmetrical in a technical sense, it certainly would have been so considered by classical Latin writers.

D.1.4. A common position for the diaeresis in the dactylic hexameter is before the fifth foot. It is called the "bucolic diaeresis" since it was felt to be a characteristic of Greek pastoral poetry.

Thus, a typical pattern showing both caesura and bucolic diaeresis might be:

$$ - \smile \smile - \smile \smile - \,||\, - - - \,||\, - \smile \smile - > $$

An example showing both is the first line of Ovid's *Metamorphosis*:

In nova fert animus || mūtātās || dīcere formās

D.1.5. Practical Implications

The implications for scansion of a line are simple, and lines can be scanned even by those who cannot determine what vowels are naturally long. A line of classical dactylic hexameter can be scanned by following a set of logical steps:

a) *The last five syllables are known:* $- \smile \smile \,|\, - >$ (D.1.1).
b) *The first syllable of the line must be long.*
c) *All syllables involving a vowel followed by two consonants are long* (A.1c).
d) *Final vowels* -o, -i, *and* -u *are nearly always long by nature* (A.1a, note).

There are a number of further steps one could take. The following are all logical consequences of the pattern of long and short syllables the hexameter requires:

a) *Any syllable falling between two long syllables is long.*
b) *Any syllable falling between two short syllables is long.*
c) *Any syllable following the combination _ ⌣ is short.*
d) *Any syllable following two short syllables is long.*

Since there are a known range of syllables in each set of feet, if after marking off, say, four feet, there are six syllables remaining, those two feet are dactyls. If there are five, what remain are a dactyl and a spondee.[5] Most important, because many hexameter lines can be accurately scanned by applying even a few of these sketchy principles it is almost pointless for non-Latinists to dwell on those lines that give problems. Even without the aid of marked long vowels, scansion of the following lines is almost mechanical:

$$\_ \; \smile \; \smile \mid \_ \; \smile \; \smile \mid \_ \; \_ \mid \_ \; \_ \mid \smile \; \smile \mid \_ \; >$$
In nova fert animus mūtātās dīcere formās
$$\_ \quad \smile \; \smile \mid \_ \; \_ \mid \_ \quad \_ \mid \_ \quad \_ \mid \smile \; \smile \mid \_ >$$
Corpora. Dī, coeptīs (nam, Dī, mūtāstis et illās)
$$\_ \quad \_ \mid \_ \; \smile \; \smile \mid \_$$
Adspīrāte meīs . . .

(Ovid, Metamorphoses 1.1–3)

[The spirit drives me to speak of forms changed into
new bodies. Gods, inspire me in these beginnings
(for you change them as well).]

See further examples in appendix (chap. 2, D.1).

D.2. Elegiac Couplet
An *elegiac couplet* is a two-line form consisting of a line of dactylic hexameter, which uses the conventions above, followed by what is often called a pentameter, which is scanned as follows:

$$\_ \; \smile \; \smile \mid \_ \; \smile \; \smile \mid \_ \parallel \_ \; \smile \; \smile \mid \_ \; \smile \; \smile \mid >$$

------

5. Another such rule pointed out to me: (total number of syllables in a line) − 12 = (number of dactyls in that line).

Each half-line in the pentameter can be called a *hemiepes*. The double vertical line corresponds to a word break; this break is generally described as a diaeresis, although it is also occasionally described as a caesura. In the pentameter, spondees may be substituted for dactyls in the first half-line; no substitution is permitted in the second half-line, and there is no necessary relation between word accent and verse accent. In contrast to the dactylic hexameter verse form, the syntax of the elegiac couplet generally supports line structure; that is, each couplet consists of a single, autonomous syntactic unit. Because this verse type was often taught in schools, examples are numerous in medieval and Renaissance Latin poetry, and it is a common form in Ovid:

> _ ˘ ˘ | _ ˘ ˘|_ ˘ ˘| _ ˘ ˘ |_ ˘ ˘ | _ >
> Parve (nec invideō) sine mē, liber, ībis in urbem:
> _ ˘ ˘ | _   ˘ ˘| _|| _ ˘ ˘|_ ˘ ˘|_
> eī mihi, quod dominō nōn licet īre tuō!
> _ ˘ ˘ | _ _ | _ _ | _ ˘ ˘|_ ˘ ˘|_ >
> vāde, sed incultus, quālem decet exulis esse:
> _ _ | _ ˘ ˘| _ || _ ˘ ˘| _ ˘ ˘| _
> infēlix habitum temporis huīus habē.
>
>   (Ovid, *Tristia*)

——————

[You will go, little book, unenvied to the city without
me; because, alas, I am not allowed to go as your master.
Go unadorned, as it is appropriate for an exile to be;
miserable, wear the habit of this age.]

E. Lyric Types (Aeolic)

The lyrics most familiar to students of classics and thus most often imitated by English poets are those of Catullus and Horace. They consist mainly of Aeolic verse forms borrowed from the Greek poets Sappho and Alcaeus and found also in Greek drama. Aeolic forms do not consist of feet, although they are occasionally analyzed in those terms. A line in Aeolic verse is characterized by an internal choriamb (_ ˘ ˘ _) preceded by what is called an Aeolic base, that is, two syllables that are anceps, either long or short. A common form is the glyconic (see sec. B.1.5 above), analyzed as follows:

X X _ ˘ ˘ _ ˘ >

The verse can be "compounded"; that is, additional syllables can precede the base. The choriambic element can also be doubled to form different line types. What is called a lesser Asclepiad adds one choriamb: x x _ ‿ ‿ _ _ ‿ ‿ _ ‿ >; and a greater Asclepiad adds two (discussed in sec. E.3.1 below). A long syllable can be resolved as two shorts in the Aeolic base, but no substitution (long for short) or resolution (two shorts for one long) is permitted after the base.

E.1. Hendecasyllable
The form of Aeolic verse associated with Catullus consists of repeating lines of eleven syllables scanned as follows: x x _ ‿ ‿ _ ‿ _ ‿ _ >. The first part of the line is a glyconic (sec. B.1.5 above).

_ _ _ ‿ ‿ _   ‿ _   ‿ _ >

Cuī dōnō lepidum novum libellum

(Catullus 1)

E.2. What are called *Sapphics* are four-line stanzas. The first three lines are hendecasyllables, scanned _ ‿ _ x _ ‿ ‿ _ ‿ _ >; these are followed by a single line scanned _ ‿ ‿ _ >. The following is the first stanza of Catullus's Latin translation of Sappho:

_ ‿ _ _ _ ‿ ‿ _ ‿ _ >

Ille mī pār esse deō vidētur

_ ‿ _ _ _   ‿ ‿ _ ‿   _ >

ille, sī fās est, superāre dīvōs

_ ‿ _ _ _ ‿ ‿ _   ‿ _ >

quī sedēns adversus identidem tē

_   ‿ ‿ _ >

spectat et audit

(Catullus 51)

[He seems to me to be like a god, or (if it is right) to surpass the gods—that man who sitting across from you sees and hears you [sweetly laughing]]

The form is also common in Horace, whose version of the Sapphic hendecasyllable has a word break following syllable 5: _ ‿ _ x _ || ‿ ‿ _ ‿ >. Metrically, the Sapphic hendecasyllable may be analyzed

as a cretic (_ ⌣ _) followed by a hipponactean (x x _ ⌣ ⌣ _ ⌣ _ _)
with a curtailed Aeolic base of one anceps (x); but the full pattern of
the line itself is easier to memorize than this somewhat dizzying formula. The Sapphic form is often imitated (visually and metrically)
by English poets.

E.3. Asclepiads
An Asclepiad is a form of Aeolic that uses one of the following four
line types:[6]

    a) *lesser Asclepiad:* x x _ ⌣ ⌣ _ _ ⌣ ⌣ _ ⌣ _
    b) *greater Asclepiad:* x x _ ⌣ ⌣ _ _ ⌣ ⌣ _ _ ⌣ ⌣ _ ⌣ _
    c) *glyconic:* x x _ ⌣ ⌣ _ ⌣ _
    d) *pherecratic:* x x _ ⌣ ⌣ _ _

E.3.1. Asclepiads are classified by types. Five Asclepiad types are found
in Horace, and other types are also possible. Scholars agree on the
forms and classifications of Asclepiads but differ on how they should
be numbered; I give Raven's numbering below, although standard
accounts vary:[7]

    I: uses a alone
    II: uses b alone
    III: four-line stanza: c, a, c, a
    IV: four-line stanza: a, a, a, c
    V: four-line stanza: a, a, d, c

Because of the rarity of substitution, the practical matter of scanning
Asclepiads for a non-Latinist requires no more than imposing upon
a four-line stanza whatever form works.

---

6. The lesser Asclepiad adds one choriamb to a glyconic; the greater Asclepiad adds two choriambs. In Horace, the syllables marked x in these Aeolic
verses are generally long. Obligatory word breaks between adjoining choriam-
bic elements in the greater and lesser Asclepiad also appear, e.g., x x _ ⌣ ⌣ _ ||
_ ⌣ ⌣ _ ⌣ _ and x x _ ⌣ ⌣ _ || _ ⌣ ⌣ _ || _ ⌣ ⌣ _ ⌣ _.

7. The numbering in the once-standard grammar of Allen and Gree-
nough is: I: a alone; II: c, a, c, a; III: a, a, a, c; IV: a, a, d, c; V: b alone. Other num-
berings include: I: a alone; II: a, a, a, c; III: a, a, d, c; IV: c, a, c, a; V: b alone.
Among additional Asclepiad types is c, c, c, d—three glyconics followed by a
pherecratic—as found in Catullus 34.

E.3.2. Example of an Asclepiad from Horace, *Odes* 1.5 (Asclepiad V in system above; variously categorized as III or IV under other systems):

x x – ˘ ˘ –|| – ˘ ˘ – ˘ –
Quis multā gracilis tē puer in rosā
x x – ˘ ˘ –|| – ˘ ˘ – ˘ >
Perfūsus liquidīs urget odōribus
x x – ˘ ˘ – –
grātō Pyrrha sub antrō?
x x – ˘˘ – ˘ >
cuī flāvam religās comam . . .

———

[What beautiful boy, fragrant in perfumes, among the roses, urges you in a welcome cave, Pyrrha, for whom do you tie your golden hair . . .]

E.4. A variant of Aeolic verse common in Horace is the *Alcaic,* a four-line stanza scanned as follows (the first two lines are a form of the hendecasyllable, with a word break after syllable 5):

x – ˘ – – || – ˘ ˘ – ˘ – (2)
x – ˘ – – – ˘ – –
– – ˘ ˘ – ˘ ˘ – ˘ – –

For an example of the Alcaic form found in Horace see appendix (chap. 2, E.4).

E.5. In the Latin Sapphics of Horace, four-line stanzas usually consist of a complete sentence and end with a full stop. In most of these Aeolic types, no relation between syntax and line and stanza structure is necessary; that is, sentence periods can continue from one stanza to the next. Thus, in Asclepiad types I–III, the four-line stanzaic unit may not be readily apparent.

F. Iambic and Trochaic Meters

These common verse types occur in two main forms: dramatic and non-dramatic. The non-dramatic form is no more complex than other meters, but the rules for the dramatic form are both difficult and controversial. In both forms, rules for substitution can involve principles of quantity (two shorts are considered equal to one long) and isosyllabism (one short syllable equals one long).[8]

F.1. Non-dramatic Forms

Basic non-dramatic forms are usually described in terms of metra rather than in terms of feet. That is, a non-dramatic twelve-syllable iambic line in Latin is conventionally called a trimeter (three four-syllable units), rather than a senarius (six two-syllable feet).

F.1.1. Iambic Trimeter

In an *iambic trimeter,* three metra of iambs are combined to form a twelve-syllable line. The basic form is as follows:

$$
\begin{array}{l}
\text{x} \qquad \_\ \smile\ \_|\text{x}\ \_\ \smile\ \_\ |\ \text{x}\ \_\ \smile\ \_ \\
\text{iam iam efficācī dō manūs scientiae} \\
\text{x}\ \_\ \ \smile\ \_\ |\ \text{x}\ \_\ \smile\ \_\ |\ \ \text{x}\ \_\ \ \smile\ \_ \\
\text{supplex et ōrō regna per Proserpinae}
\end{array}
$$

(Horace, Epodes 17)

――――

[Now, I give my hands as a suppliant to efficacious knowledge and pray through the realms of Proserpina]

Substitutions: The first syllable of each four-syllable metron can be long or short. Two shorts can be substituted for a long in any but the last position. There is generally a word break after the fifth syllable.

F.1.2. A trochaic example of non-dramatic verse is the *catalectic trochaic tetrameter.* This line has four metra, each consisting of two trochees; the last syllable is lacking (catalectic). The final syllable of each metron can be long or short, and a break (in this case diaeresis) generally occurs after syllable 8. The basic form is as follows:

――――――――

8. Paradoxically, this was the form most familiar to early schoolboys, who used phrasebooks made out of the dialogue of Terence. Some editions of these phrasebooks and early printed editions of Terence as well show that their readers and editors were unaware of or indifferent to the fact that Terence was in verse.

$$- \smile - \text{x} - \smile - \text{x} \mid - \smile - \text{x} - \smile -$$

In this example from Seneca's *Phaedrus,* ordinary substitutions are seen in metron 1: the long in position 3 is resolved as two shorts; the anceps syllable in position 4 is long:

$$- \quad \smile \; \smile \; \smile - \mid - \; \smile \; - \quad - \mid - \quad \smile \; - \; - \mid - \quad \smile \; >$$
morte facilī dignus haud sum quī novā nātum nece

There are no restrictions on substitutions, but there are generally, in any given group of lines, fewer such substitutions than in the comparable iambic line (sec. F.1.1 above).[9]

F.2. Dramatic Forms
In Latin, the dramatic versions of iambic and trochaic lines are described in terms of feet, not metra, and the same rules of substitution apply to each foot (in non-dramatic forms of iambics, substitutions are not permitted in even-numbered feet).

F.2.1. The most common dramatic line type is the *iambic senarius.* The basic form is as follows:

$$\text{x} - \mid \text{x} - \mid \text{x} - \mid \text{x} - \mid \text{x} - \mid \smile -$$

x is anceps; thus it can be either long or short, producing two possibilities for each foot: $\smile -$ and $- -$. However, any long syllable may be resolved as two short syllables. Thus any of the following foot types are possible: $\smile -$, $\smile \smile \smile$, $- -$, $- \smile \smile$, $\smile \smile -$, and $\smile \smile \smile \smile$. This line type seems to admit nearly anything, but examination shows the following feet are not permitted: $- \smile$, $- \smile -$, etc. In addition, rules governing exceptions, such as brevis brevians, operate more freely, and many long syllables can be shortened that would not be shortened in

---

9. The catalectic trochaic tetrameter is indistinguishable from what in dramatic verse is called trochaic septenarius (sec. F.2.2 below). Note that the diaeresis in the trochaic line produces the same metrical scheme following it as does the caesura in the comparable iambic line.

other verse. In general, scanning even basic lines is not a reasonable thing to ask of anyone other than a skilled Latinist:

$$\breve{\ }\ {-}|\breve{\ }\ {-}\ |\ {-}\qquad\breve{\ }\ \breve{\ }\ |\qquad{-}\qquad{-}|\ {-}\qquad{-}\ |\ \breve{\ }\ {>}$$

Poëta quom prīmum animum ad scrībendum adpulit,

(Terence, *Eunuchus*)

For additional examples see appendix (chap. 2, F.2).

F.2.2. The second most common dramatic line is the *catalectic trochaic septenarius:* seven feet of trochees; the last syllable is dropped. A diaeresis usually occurs after the fourth foot, which makes the last half of the line metrically identical to the last half of an iambic senarius (see sec. F.1.2, note 9). The same substitutions that are found in the iambic senarius are permitted, but they are less frequent. The form is often seen at the end of Terence's plays:

$$\breve{\ }\ \breve{\ }\ \breve{\ }|\ {-}\ {-}\ |\ {-}\qquad{-}\ |\ {-}\qquad\breve{\ }\ |\ {-}\ \breve{\ }\ |\ {-}\qquad{-}\ |\ {-}\ \breve{\ }\ |\ {-}$$

Ego deōrum vītam eampropter sempiternam esse arbitror.

(Terence, *Andria*)

F.2.3. Other iambic and trochaic dramatic meters include the *iambic septenarius* (seven feet of iambs), the *trochaic octonarius* (eight feet of trochees), and many other forms. Since various forms can be mixed, almost arbitrarily, even in a single passage of dialogue, most editions of Terence or Plautus come with an index of meters.[10]

G. Epode

In classical Latin and Greek verse, the possible combinations of feet and verse types are numerous: lines can be built based on anapests,

---

10. Modern editions conventionally identify the meter of each line, and some mark the *ictus* of each metron, thus in the example from section F.2.2 above, the first element of each four-syllable metron: "Égo deorum vítam eampropter sémpiternam esse árbitror." Even with such aids, non-Latinists and Latinists alike may have difficulty with these lines.

bacchiacs, or even cretics. Of special note is the *epode*. The general definition of an epode is a distich of two lines formed of line types that often use different metrical bases. Among many variants in Horace is a couplet formed with a line of dactylic hexameter followed by an iambic line:

$$\_ \ \smile \ \smile \ | \_ \ \_ \ | \_ \ \_ | \_ \ \_ | \ \_ \ \smile \ \smile \ | \_ >$$

Nox erat et caelō fulgēbat Lūna serēnō

$$x \ \_ \ | \ x \ \_ \ | \ x \ \_ \ | \ \smile >$$

inter minōra sīdera

(Horace, *Epodes* 15)

———

[It was night, and the moon shone in the clear sky among the lesser stars]

H. Cantica

Found in the plays of Plautus, the *cantica* is a long form that consists of irregular mixtures of rhythmic patterns and types. It may be dominated by a verse type (or type of foot), although this is not a necessary criterion of the form. What appear to be individual stanzas or units are potentially repeatable but are not necessarily repeated in the text.[11] Thus, in any cantica, no line structure can be predicted from the structure of the preceding line, and this is tantamount to saying that no abstract analysis is possible apart from specific examples.

———

Texts: All texts are adapted from Oxford Classical Texts editions; all translations are mine.

References: Joseph H. Allen, J. B. Greenough, et al., *Allen and Greenough's New Latin Grammar for Schools and Colleges* (1888; numerous re-editions); D. S. Raven, *Latin Metre: An Introduction* (London: Faber and Faber, 1965). James W. Halporn, Martin Ostwald, and Thomas G. Rosenmeyer, *The Meters of Greek and Latin Poetry* (1980; rev. ed. Indianapolis: Hackett, 1994); M. L. West, *Introduction to Greek Metre* (Oxford: Clarendon Press, 1987).

———

11. Latin cantica do not follow the common Greek form, which consists of a repeating three-stanza unit of strophe, antistrophe, epode (where strophe and antistrophe are metrically identical).

Chapter Three

Syllabic Verse

French

A. *Basic Principles*
B. *Basic Verse Types*
C. *Caesura*
D. *Rhythmic Features*
E. *Assonance*
F. *Rhyme Types*
G. *Fixed Forms*

A. Basic Principles

A.1. In syllabic or isosyllabic verse (the terms are effectively synonymous), the verse line is defined strictly in terms of number of syllables. Theoretically, lines of any length are possible, although metricians claim that lines over eight syllables must have other features, such as internal caesurae or regular stress patterns, to be metrically intelligible to listeners. French twelve-syllable lines are thus in units of six syllables; some longer English verses are organized by accentual rhythms. In purely syllabic or isosyllabic verse, only the number of syllables matters, and there are no supplemental rules regarding accent or quantity. Examples in English include the verse experiments of Marianne Moore and Robert Bridges (chap. 6, B.2). Classical French verse, although usefully classified as syllabic or isosyllabic, incorporates supplemental rules of accent.

A.1.1. Most histories of French verse distinguish major periods and schools as follows: Old and Middle French (1100–1500); Grands

Rhétoriqueurs (1460–1520); Pléiade (sixteenth-century; major figures include Ronsard and DuBellay); classicists (seventeenth and eighteenth centuries; major figures include Malherbe, Corneille, Racine, Boileau); Romantics (Hugo, Baudelaire); Moderns (Verlaine, Apollinaire). These schools differ on various details of versification: rhymes or scansions that are accepted in the nineteenth century might not be accepted in the seventeenth century; others might be rejected as old-fashioned. All agree, however, on two basic principles: (1) French verse is isosyllabic, in the sense that the foundation for the line is a particular number of syllables that are not distinguished in terms of accent or syllable length; (2) the definition of syllable and even of rhyme is conventional; that is, the prosodic syllable is not a matter of phonetics or a function of the way the language is spoken.

A.1.2. French literature has a conservative and self-conscious critical history. Many details in Eustaches Deschamps' *Art de Dictier,* a treatise on poetic form in the late Middle Ages, are applicable to nineteenth-century French verse; and many of the innovations of modern French verse are based on modifications of classical rules and conventions.

A.2. Metrics vs. Stylistics
The difference between metrics and stylistics is an important one, and I have tried to limit my discussion below to metrics, that is, rule-bound features that are fundamental to verse. A metrical rule determines the difference between what might be called "legal" and "illegal" verse, whereas a stylistic rule might distinguish a "good" verse from a "bad" one.

A.2.1. Discussions of French meter often conflate metrics and stylistics, beginning with such considerations as *rhythm.* Rhythm, difficult to define, includes such features as grammatical structure, secondary accent, even rhetorical and performative elements forming the phrase structure of individual lines. However basic these elements might seem, they tend toward the level of stylistics, that is, they are not matters of rules of versification. Furthermore, one cannot analyze such elements without more than a basic knowledge of the language (see sec. D.1 below on the flexible and movable *coupe*).

A.3. Definitions

A.3.1. Syllable

Syllables in classical French verse are not defined phonetically, and the number of syllables in spoken French is not the same as the number of syllables in verse. French verse defines syllables as they were pronounced during the early history of French as spelling was formalized. This means that a syllable is defined roughly as the syllable represented by the word's spelling. The word *chose,* for example, is in spoken French one syllable (it has what is called terminal e-mute). In verse, this terminal -*e* counts as a syllable, and the word has two syllables.[1]

A.3.1.1. The opening line of "Bénédiction" from Baudelaire's *Fleurs du Mal* might be pronounced as ten syllables. In verse, it has thirteen: *lorsque* is two syllables (one in spoken French); *puissances* three, *suprêmes* also three (both have two syllables in spoken French). In my representations below, I use a lowercase x to represent one verse syllable.

    x   x x x   x x x   x x x x x x
    Lorsque, par un décret des puissances suprêmes

A.3.1.2. Internal -*e*-, ordinarily not pronounced in spoken French, has full syllabic value in verse, unless it follows an unaccented vowel: thus *ornement* counts as three full syllables, as does *flamboiements* (-*e*- does not constitute a syllable).

A.3.2. Vowel Combinations

Certain vowel combinations are diphthongs, that is, they count as one syllable. Others are disyllabic. Among the more common diphthongs are *ai, au, eu, eau, oi.* Some vowel combinations can count as one or two syllables: *ie, ien, io, ue,* and *ui.*

---

1. The definition of a syllable is defended vigorously by Mazaleyrat, who notes (1) verse is based legitimately on "illusions" rather than phonetic realities and (2) the classical definition of syllable permits a balance between consonant and vowel, one represented by the spelling of early French. The evolution of the language, involving the dropping of unstressed, post-tonic vowels, for example, reduces this balance by emphasizing the consonants. See Mazaleyrat, pp. 31–36.

A.3.2.1. The basis for this pronunciation or prosodic value is often etymological: if the French word comes from a Latin word where the two vowels were separated or pronounced as two syllables, the modern French word is generally a disyllable: *lion* from *leo; suer* from *sudare*. If the French vowels evolve from a single Latin vowel, the monosyllabic pronunciation is retained: *fait* from *factum* (the French -*ai*- is formed from the Latin -*a*-); *fier* from *ferus* (the French -*ie*- is formed from the Latin -*e*-). Old French terminations -*ions*, -*iez* of the imperfect are disyllabic. In Modern French, these same endings are prosodically monosyllabic, but if preceded by a mute consonant (*p, t, k,* etc.) plus a liquid (*l* or *r*), they are disyllabic (for these consonant combinations in Latin, see chap. 2, A.1). The disyllabic pronunciation is called *diaeresis* (e.g., *pri-ons*); the monosyllabic pronunciation is called *syneresis* (e.g., *all-ions*). Many cases are controversial: *ei* preceded by mute plus liquid is often disyllabic; *pleinne* thus can have three syllables (so Corneille); the Academy claimed this should be two.

A.3.2.2. However abstruse these rules, for readers of classical French poetry, even those with minimal knowledge of French, the words involved pose more difficulties in theory than in practice; the required number of syllables in a line will determine how such syllables are counted.

A.3.3. Pronunciation
In all cases, to say how a word is pronounced in verse refers only to its status in the composition of verse (for example, does a particular unit count as a syllable or does it not count as a syllable? does it qualify as a rhyme?); there are no absolute rules or conventions governing how readers of verse (whether professional actors performing classical drama or amateurs) are to pronounce these lines.

A.4. Tonic Accent
Multisyllabic French words have one primary accent, which in spoken French occurs on the final syllable. This is called the *tonic accent*. Elements following this accent, generally grammatical inflections, are not pronounced in spoken French but count as full syllables in French verse. In the line above, two words that are disyllabic in speech are trisyllabic in verse: puis-SANC-es, su-PRÊM-es. In speech, the terminal -*es* would not be pronounced.

A.4.1. The most common grammatical inflection is a final, unaccented *-e*, conventionally called e-mute, or e-*caduc*, and special rules apply for its treatment. For plural feminine nouns and adjectives, this terminal *-e* becomes *-es*. In spoken French, *blanche* and *blanches* are monosyllabic and indistinguishable; in French verse, they are disyllabic and the terminal *-s* in the plural is sounded (but see qualifications above, sec. A.3.3). The word accent remains the same in spoken and poetic French.

A.4.1.1. Non-French speakers can easily determine the position of the accent in regard to e-mute endings by a simple convention of orthography. For any multisyllabic word, a terminal *-e* or *-es* that is pronounced in spoken French receives the word accent, and that accent will be noted typographically with an acute accent. If there is no printed accent on such a termination, then the ending is mute in spoken French and in verse constitutes a "post-tonic" syllable, that is, the accent is on the preceding syllable. Thus *bonté* is disyllabic both in speech and in verse, with a terminal accent on the *é; conte* is monosyllabic in speech, but disyllabic in verse, with the tonic accent on the first element: CONT-e.

A.4.2. Similar to the e-mute are certain other inflectional endings: for example, the terminal *-ent* in the word *confondent,* the third person plural of the verb *confonder* [to confound]. In speech, this *-ent* is not pronounced and the word has two syllables; in verse, the final *-ent* is pronounced but the accent remains on the preceding syllable.

A.5. Basic Definition of Verse Line

A line in most French verse is defined (or counted) in terms of the final tonic accent in that line. Thus a decasyllabic line is defined as a line with a final, tonic accent on syllable 10; an Alexandrine as a line with a final, tonic accent on syllable 12. Since unaccented inflectional endings may follow this tonic accent, the actual number of syllables in a given line can be greater.

A.5.1. For most lines in French, the scansion is purely mechanical and is no more difficult for those who do not know French than for those who do; in lines of twelve syllables, there is a terminal accent on syllable 12 (I represent this accent with an uppercase X).

```
x      x x x    x x   x   x   x x    x  X x
```
Lorsque, par un décret des puissances suprêmes,

This is a twelve-syllable line (an Alexandrine). If this same line were spoken, there would be ten syllables (although this would depend on the treatment of *-que* in *Lorsque*):

```
x          x  x   x x   x x    x      x    x
```
Lorsq(ue), par un décret des puissanc(es) suprêm(es)

A.6. Elision
As in Latin, French verse has rules of *elision*. In verse, post-tonic terminal syllables ending in vowels are elided when followed by words beginning with a vowel. Thus the phrase "ventre a conçu" below:

```
x    x  x  x   x   x x    x xx xX
```
Où mon ventre a conçu mon expiation!
(Baudelaire, "Bénédiction")

The terminal *-e* in *ventre*, normally pronounced in verse, is elided: "ventr(e) a". In the phrase "Elle ravale ainsi" the *-e* in *Elle* is counted as a syllable, but the *-e* in *ravale* is elided due to the following *ainsi*.

A.6.1. Elision does not occur in certain line positions of particular verse types. Post-tonic vowels at the end of the line are not elided with the beginning of the next line. In some medieval verse, a post-tonic vowel at the mid-line caesura would also not be elided (see sec. C.1.2 below on epic caesura).

A.6.2. In chapter 2, I treated *hiatus* as the exception to elision in classical Latin and Greek verse. For French verse, hiatus is more important. Linguistically, hiatus is the break between two vowels (in a single word, *nu-ée*). For French verse, the most important case is the pause between the terminal and initial vowels of succeeding words in such common phrases as "tu a," "ni elle," "ou on," etc. In classical French verse, these combinations are generally not permitted. In pre-classical French verse, hiatus involving a terminal and initial vowel was permitted only at the caesura (a conventional mid-line break), as in this line by Ronsard:

Je n'ay jamais servi || autres maistres que rois.

The phrase "servi autres" would not be permitted in classical French verse.

A.7. Further Consequences of Classical Rules

For most words, the classical rules of French verse are unproblematic: the word *monde,* normally pronounced as a monosyllable, is pronounced as two syllables in verse. But for certain words the difference between normal pronunciation and syllable count in verse became intolerable to French sensibility, for example, feminine nouns and adjectives whose singular ends in accented *-ée*. In spoken French, the endings *-é, -ée* and their plurals *-és, -ées* are identical in pronunciation. Under the strict rules of verse, a word such as *nuée* [cloud], or its plural *nuées,* should be three syllables (nu-E-e). But pronouncing this final syllable, as the rules of classical prosody would require, produces two examples of hiatus. The rule was thus established that these words could only be used at the end of a line, or if the final *-e* could be elided with the following word. Thus, the pronunciation *nu-é-es* was avoided (or seemed to be avoided). And one set of artificial rules (the pronunciation of a mute *-e*) was trumped (or salvaged) by another (post-vocalic e-mute could only be used in cases where it would not have to be pronounced).

A.7.1. French "clouds" thus only appear at the end of a French line, never in the middle. And there are no "white clouds" (*des nuées blanches*) anywhere to be found in French classical verse simply because there are no positions in French decasyllabic or Alexandrine verse where such a common phrase would be metrically acceptable.

A.7.2. Many other common words also cannot be used in the interior of the verse. The plural *vies* ("lives," sing. *vie*) cannot appear except in the final position of a line, because by rule the terminal, post-tonic element (*-es*) ought to be elided but cannot be elided due to the final *-s*.

B. Basic Verse Types

B.1. The earliest systematic treatises on French verse in the Middle Ages analyzed verse types according to the number of syllables in a line and recognized lines from one to fourteen syllables in length. Victor Hugo acknowledges this tradition in his poem "Les Djinns," written in a stanza formed of lines of two, three, four, five, six, seven, eight, and ten syllables. One curious phenomenon in French is that stanzas with lines of an odd number of syllables tend to be based on music, and this feature is also worth checking for certain early English verses as well (e.g., in the songs of John Donne, chap. 6, D).

B.2. The line types that have received the most critical attention in French verse are those of eight, ten, and twelve syllables, that is, those showing an even number of syllables. The octosyllable, generally in rhymed couplets, was a standard form for much narrative verse in Old French (chivalric romances, beast epics, *fabliaux*). The decasyllable was used in *ballades,* courtly stanzaic forms, and some epic poems (*Chanson de Roland*). Certain military epics (*chansons de geste*) were in stanzas composed of twelve-syllable lines (Alexandrines). The word *Alexandrine* is derived from the twelfth-century epic on Alexander the Great composed in such lines.

B.2.1. Octosyllable
The *octosyllable* is a line with a terminal accent on syllable 8. There are generally no required breaks in mid line. The most common form is in rhymed couplets.

> La damoisele estoit si bien
> de sa dame, que nule rien
> a dire ne li redotast
> a quoi que la chose montast.
>   (Chrétien de Troyes,
>   *Lancelot* [twelfth century])

B.2.2. Decasyllable
A *decasyllable* is a line with a terminal accent on syllable 10. This terminal accent may be followed by one (or theoretically more than one) unaccented syllable, a syllable that would not be pronounced in modern French pronunciation. Thus a decasyllabic line has the basic metrical form:

x x x x x x x x x X (x)

Most decasyllabic lines will have a real or implied break following syllable 4:

> De mon vrai cuer || jamais ne partira
> L'impression || de vo douce figure
> (Machaut, *Le Livre du voir dit*)

A few medieval variants of the decasyllable show this break following syllable 6, dividing the line 6/4, as in *Aiol,* a thirteenth-century *chanson de geste.* Other decasyllables are without a caesura.

B.2.2.1. *Italian Variants.* The French decasyllable has the same form as the Italian hendecasyllable (eleven-syllable line), the most basic line in Italian poetry. An Italian hendecasyllable is defined exactly as is the French decasyllable: a line with a terminal accent on syllable 10. Because of the nature of Italian grammar and prosody, most of these lines will in fact be of eleven syllables; some will be of ten and others of twelve syllables.

> x   x x x   x   x   x   x   x X x
> Nel mezzo del cammin per nostra vita
> x x   x x   x x x x   x X x
> Mi ritrovai per una selva oscura
> (Dante, *Inferno*)

B.2.3. Alexandrine
The Alexandrine is the most important line in French literary history. It is defined as a line of twelve or more syllables with a terminal accent on syllable 12. The classical Alexandrine shows a caesura following accented syllable 6 and the line itself consists then of two *hemistiches.*

> x x x x   x   X ||x   x   x   x x X x
> La sottise, l'erreur, le péché, la lésine
> (Baudelaire, "Bénédiction")

C. Caesura

In French verse, a caesura is a mid-line syntactic break. The caesura cannot appear, for example, in the middle of a prepositional phrase or between a subject pronoun and verb. It is not the same as the caesura defined in Latin verse (see chap. 2, B.2). All classical forms of the Alexandrine have some kind of caesura and strict rules regarding its placement. Many forms of decasyllabic verse have a caesura as well. In the classical Alexandrine, the caesura regularly follows syllable 6. In the decasyllable, the most common form of caesura follows an accented syllable 4. I represent it here with a double vertical line (||). In many analyses of verse, it is represented by a single or double virgule (/ or //).

C.1. Theoretical Forms of the Caesura: Classical, Epic, Lyric

The most common form of caesura is the *classical caesura,* which immediately follows a mid-line terminal tonic accent. Two other forms, associated largely with medieval verse, are the *epic caesura* and the *lyric caesura.* These occur when the caesura follows an unaccented terminal syllable. If that syllable is counted in the line analysis, the caesura is a lyric caesura; if it is not counted, the caesura is an epic caesura.

C.1.1. Classical Caesura

In the Alexandrine, the classical caesura divides the line into two six-syllable hemistiches:

> x x x x x X   x x x   x x   X x
> Nos péchés sont têtus, || nos repentirs sont lâches.
>   (Baudelaire, "Au lecteur")

Decasyllabic verse is rare after the medieval period, but Ronsard in "Des Amours" shows regular, classical caesura after syllable 4 (marked in the lines below):

> Ces diamans, || ces rubis, qu'un Zephyre
> Tient animez || d'un soupir adouci,
> Et ces oeillets || et ces roses aussi,
> Et ce fin or, || où l'or mesme se mire . . .

C.1.2. Epic Caesura

The epic caesura is a basic form of caesura found in the eleventh-century *Chanson de Roland* and elsewhere. In *Roland,* each line has a

caesura following the tonic accent on syllable 4. If an unaccented terminal syllable follows the tonic accent, the terminal syllable is disregarded; it is not counted in the scansion and is treated thus exactly
as such a syllable would be treated at the end of a line. The second
line below shows epic caesura and thus an extra, uncounted syllable
in the first half-line.

> x   x   x   X ‖ x   x   x   x   x   X
> Co sent Rollanz   que la mort le tresprent,
> x x   x   X x ‖ x   x   x   x   x   X
> de vers la teste   sur le quer li descent.

>   -----

> [Roland sensed that death held him,
> It descended from the head to the heart.]

A poem that shows epic caesura will generally show epic caesura in
all cases of unaccented syllables at the caesura.[2]

C.1.3. Lyric Caesura

A lyric caesura is defined as a caesura following an unaccented element that does count in the overall scansion of the line and half-line.
To my knowledge, this caesura is only found in decasyllabic verse.
The difference between the epic caesura and lyric caesura involves
(1) whether the terminal element is counted, and (2) the placement
of the tonic accent. In *Chanson de Roland,* the tonic accent is always
on syllable 4. But in decasyllabic lines with lyric caesura, the tonic accent necessarily appears in syllable 3. The following example is from
Le Châtelain de Coucy (fourteenth century).

> x   x   X   x ‖ x   x   x   x   x X
> Mais ma dame ‖ ne quiert si mon mal non.
>   (Quoted by Kastner, p. 87)

   -----

2. It is inconvenient to speak of the post-tonic syllable as syllable 5, since
the basic structure of each line has a second tonic accent at what I call syllable
10. Therefore, I continue to speak of the initial syllable following the caesura
in such lines as syllable 5.

Most poems that show lyric caesura use it infrequently. The two types of caesura, lyric and epic, are generally not found in the same poem.

C.2. Special Problems of the Caesura in Decasyllable
The definitions of caesura types are not controversial, but determining whether an apparent case is metrical, purely stylistic, or even accidental can be problematic. The lyric caesura does not appear regularly in decasyllable verse; and many poems that seem to show evidence of such a caesura might be better analyzed as having, rather than any caesura, an arbitrary (stylistic) pattern of phrasal breaks.

C.2.1. Most decasyllabic lines in French show caesura after syllable 4, and in the classical form, this syllable will also show a tonic accent. Only if the entire poem shows a pattern of regular caesurae can the exceptional lyric caesura be claimed. If the word *caesura* is used in the description of individual lines, it is merely a stylistic term, not a metrical one. That is, it does not refer to the overall composition of the poem.

C.2.2. Froissart, *Flour de la margherite,* shows regular (classical) caesura:

> Blanche et vermeille, ‖ et par usage habite
> en tous vers lieus, ‖ aillours ne se delite.
> ossi chier ‖ a le preel d'un hermite,
> mes qu'elle y puist ‖ croistre sans opposite.

Note in the first line, the *-e* of *vermeille* at the caesura is elided.

C.2.3. Deschamps, in his *Ballades,* shows an example of lyric caesura:

> He! gens d'armes, ‖ aiez en remembrance
> vostre pere, ‖ vous estiez si enfant,
> le bon Bertran, ‖ qui tant ot de puissance,
> qui vous amoit ‖ si amoureusement,
> Guesclin prioit . . .

Here, a word break appears without exception after syllable 4, and the invocation of lyric caesura in lines 1 and 2 is surely legitimate.

C.2.4. Machaut, *Dit de la harpe*:

> Phebus, un dieus de moult haute puissance,
> avoit la harpe en si grant reverence
> que chans nouviaus ja ne li eschapast,
> qu'en la harpe ne jouast ne harpast.
> par dessus tous instrumens la prisoit
> et envers li tous autres desprisoit.

The first three lines could be analyzed as showing regular caesura, preceded by an accent on syllable 4. But despite the word breaks between syllables 4 and 5 in the following lines, it is pointless to speak of caesura here (and clearly incorrect to claim one exists between the definite article *li* and its noun phrase *tous autres* in the final line). If one were to cite line 4 as exhibiting lyric caesura following "qu'en la harpe," one has reduced the caesura from a metrical to a purely stylistic element. These lines have no regular caesura of any kind.

C.2.5. Conventional Accent at Syllable 4

French decasyllables tend to have tonic accent on syllable 4, which leads to an apparent caesura. But this is not the same as a caesura that exists by convention or rule. It is in my view inaccurate in terms of French verse to speak of a flexible caesura or occasional caesura in such cases if these line-structures are produced by accident or, say, by the simple use of common phrases at the beginning of a decasyllable:

> Dans les caveaux d'insondable tristesse
> Où le Destin m'a déjà relégué;
> Où jamais n'entre un rayon rose et gai;
> Où, seul avec la Nuit, maussade hôtesse . . .
>   (Baudelaire, "Un Fantôme")

The implied caesura in the first three lines is only apparent, as the following line from the same poem indicates:

> Je suis comme un peintre qu'un Dieu moqueur

There is clearly no syntactic break between the article *un* and the noun *peintre*, and the word break alone does not constitute a caesura.

C.2.6. Italian Variants

The Italian hendecasyllable is defined exactly as is the French deca-syllable (sec. B.2.2.1 above). Conventionally, Italian hendecasyllables are said to have an accent on either syllable 4 or 6 along with a flexible caesura. But Italian verse does not show a regular caesura, and it is better to drop this term. To claim that Italian verse has a flexible or movable caesura is to concede that such caesurae exist only in a sty-listic and not in a metrical sense.

C.2.7. English Variants

English variants differ from Italian variants in that they are modeled directly upon the French; they do not simply evolve from the same source as French and Italian. Chaucer's decasyllables are modeled after medieval French decasyllables; more controversially, Pope's decasyllables are heavily influenced by the rules of classical French Alexandrines. The caesura, regular after syllable 4 in both, is likely a reflection of these sources or a direct allusion to these sources. See below, chapter 6, B.

C.3. The Caesura in the Classical Alexandrine

Classical Alexandrines show caesura following a required tonic ac-cent in syllable 6, and the line itself consists of two hemistiches. Thus the full description of an Alexandrine line is as follows:

$$x \; x \; x \; x \; x \; X \parallel x \; x \; x \; x \; x \; X \; (x)$$

Note that the two halves of the line are not quite the same.

C.3.1.

In nearly all periods of French verse, a line could end in an unaccented syllable, that is, a post-tonic syllable. But if a post-tonic syllable were to occur at the caesura (following syllable 4 of a decasyl-lable or syllable 6 of an Alexandrine), it would have to be accounted for in some way. Theoretically, the post-tonic syllable could count either as one of the required number of syllables (lyric caesura) or as an extra syllable in that position (epic caesura). For the latter, a rule similar to rules in French permitting an extra syllable at the end of a line would need to apply to the caesura.

C.3.2. Classical Solution

Classical Alexandrines generally do not permit epic or lyric caesura. That is, a post-tonic *-e* can neither count as one of the six syllables required of the first hemistich, nor serve as an extra syllable. But post-tonic vowels inevitably appear at the caesura, and the classical solution seems almost desperate.

C.3.2.1. In classical Alexandrines, post-tonic syllables are permitted at the caesura, as they are in medieval verse, *but only if elided.* If the word preceding the caesura has a post-tonic syllable, that syllable must be elided with the word immediately following the caesura, a word which necessarily must begin with a vowel.

> Nous volons au passage || un plaisir clandestin
> (Baudelaire, "Au lecteur")
>
> ─────
>
> [We steal a clandestine pleasure in passing]

The word *passage* is permitted in this position because it is followed by a word beginning with a vowel, and the *-e* is elided. So also:

> Dans nos cerveaux ribote || un peuple de Démons.
>
> ─────
>
> [A demon nation riots in our heads]

The *-e* in *ribote* is elided.

C.3.3. Consequences

To most English readers, the rules of the caesura in classical Alexandrines may seem a case of establishing one set of arbitrary rules, then a second set of equally arbitrary rules to eliminate the occasional inconvenient consequences of the first set. Further reflection will show that many common words cannot be used at the caesura. For example, a feminine noun or adjective ending in *-es* cannot be used because the post-tonic ending (*-es*) cannot be elided (see sec. A.4 above).

C.4. History of Caesura

C.4.1. One of the most striking of the many changes in French verse in the nineteenth century involves the definition of the caesura. Most histories of French versification state that Victor Hugo changed the conventional structure of the Alexandrine into a three-part (ternary) line. Thus with Hugo the Alexandrine began to show three phrasal units rather than two hemistiches. I mark these implied breaks with a single virgule in the lines below:

> Je marcherai / les yeux fixés / sur mes pensées
> Sans rien voir au-dehors, sans entendre aucun bruit,
> Seul, inconnu, / le dos courbé, / les mains croisés,
> Triste, et le jour pour moi sera comme la nuit.
> > (Hugo, "Demain, dès l'aube à
> > l'heur où blanchit la campagne")

———

> [I will walk, my eyes fixed on my thoughts
> Seeing nothing outside, hearing no noise,
> Alone, unknown, my back bent, my hands folded,
> Sad, and the day for me will be like the night.]

But in Hugo's Alexandrines, all ternary lines can also be analyzed as having classical caesura following syllable 6, even though the phrase structure opposes it (e.g., "les yeux || fixés," "le dos || courbé"):

> Je marcherai les yeux || fixés sur mes pensées
> Sans rien voir au-dehors, || sans entendre aucun bruit,
> Seul, inconnu, le dos || courbé, les mains croisés,
> Triste, et le jour pour moi || sera comme la nuit.

This ternary Alexandrine became known as the romantic Alexandrine.

C.4.2. A greater challenge to the domination of the Alexandrine was by Verlaine, who wrote lines that looked like Alexandrines according to a completely different (and arbitrary) set of rules: thirteen-syllable lines, eleven-syllable lines, twelve-syllable lines without caesura. These are unlike free verse, in that each is produced according to strict rules (even though Verlaine may have made up those rules in the process of composition). Such artificial rules could produce phrases for which there was no precedent in French verse. An example is Verlaine's "Langueur," in twelve-syllable lines with no caesura:

> Je suis l'Empire à la fin de la décadence,
> Qui regarde passer les grands Barbares blancs
> En composant des acrostiches indolents
> D'un style d'or où la langueur du soleil danse.

> [I am the Empire at the end of its decadence,
> who watches the great white barbarians pass,
> while composing indolent acrostics
> in a golden style where the languor of the sun dances.]

D. Rhythmic Features

D.1. *Coupe* and Measure

A word currently receiving more use in the study of French metrics is *coupe*. A *coupe* is a phrasal break, and in earliest French treatises, this word was used to describe what is now a caesura. In modern manuals, the word is used to define those breaks implied by basic phrase structure. Units bounded by *coupes* are often called *measures*. Thus, most Alexandrines will show a caesura dividing two hemistiches, and within each of those hemistiches, a *coupe* separating two phrasal units, or measures.

D.1.1. When classical Alexandrines are analyzed this way, the *coupe* is a secondary break, as in the following line of Rousseau analyzed by Mazaleyrat (p. 15):

> Rien n'y garde / une form(e) ‖ constante / et arrêté

In this case, one must define the caesura as the basic structural break, the *coupe* as a supplemental break. In the above line, the caesura defines two hemistiches; a *coupe* within each hemistich defines one as 4/2, the other as 3/3.

D.1.2. When the word *coupe* is used to indicate the phrasal structure of romantic and modern French verse, its relation to the caesura is less clear, as in the line from Hugo quoted above:

Je marcherai / les yeux fixés / sur mes pensées.

The two *coupes* here are used to define the basic three-part structure of the line. The caesura (between *yeux* and *fixés*) is not part of the basic line structure. In other lines, the caesura is in fact part of the basic structure. Mazaleyrat (p. 20) analyzes lines from Apollinaire's "d'Alcoöls" as follows:

S'étendant / sur les côtés / du cimetière
La maison / des morts // l'encadrait / comme un cloître.

———

[Extending over the sides of the cemetery
The house of the dead frames it like a cloister.]

In this case, I assume the implied caesura in line 2 is considered part of the phrase structure, and Mazaleyrat considers the basic structure of these lines as 3 / 4 / 4 and 3/2 // 3/3.

D.2. Rhythm
What is called the *rhythm* of a French line, however defined, is a function of the accents and phrasal units that form *measures* whose boundaries are defined as *coupes*. So considered, rhythm is directly related to the analysis by measure or *coupe*. No doubt these features are self-consciously used by French poets, but they belong, in my view, to the realm of stylistics rather than metrics. That is, the placement of a phrasal *coupe* is not something required by rules of versification, but something preferred by considerations of style. Georges Lote has pointed out that there is no mention of accent or its relation to rhythm in any commentary on French verse before the eighteenth century.

D.3. Enjambment (*Rejet/contre-rejet*)
Classical Alexandrines generally form autonomous syntactic units corresponding to each line. Where they do not, one speaks of *en-*

jambment. Most metricians consider the elements known as *rejet* and *contre-rejet* as two special cases of enjambment. The following two examples, shown here in italics, should suffice (both examples from Mazaleyrat, pp. 120–23):

> C'est ici que l'amour, la grâce, la beauté,
> *La jeunesse* ont fixé leurs demeures fidèles.
>   (Chénier, "Fragments d'élegies," XXI)
>
> ———
>
> [It is here that love, grace, beauty,
> and youth have fixed their faithful homes.]

La jeunesse, which belongs to the preceding syntactic phrase, is characterized as the *rejet*.

> Plus loin, des ifs taillés en triangle. *La lune*
> D'un soir d'été sur tout cela.
>   (Verlaine, "Nuit de Walpurgis classique")
>
> ———
>
> [Further off, the yews cut in a triangle. The moon
> of a summer evening over all.]

La lune, which belongs to the following phrase, is characterized as the *contre-rejet*. These features may be more a matter of stylistics than metrics.

E. Assonance

Assonance is only a metrical matter in early medieval verse, specifically the *chansons de geste,* which are written in stanzas called *laisses*. The final syllable in each line of a *laisse* must have the same vowel sound, and lines are thus organized by such assonance rather than rhyme.

> ço dist li quens "or sai jo veirem*ent*
> que hoi murrum par le mien esc*ï*ent.
> ferez! Franceis, car jol vus recum*enz*."
> dist Oliviers: "dehet ait li plus l*enz!*"
>   (*Chanson de Roland*)

The italicized terminations are linked by the nasalized *-e*, which constitutes the assonance (such sounds as *-ent* and *-enz* do not properly rhyme).

> As vus Rollant sur sun cheval pasm*e*t,
> e Olivers ki est a mort naffr*e*z. . . .
> si li demandet dulcement e su*ë*f
> "sire cumpain, faites le vos de gr*e*d? . . ."

The lines are linked by terminal assonance on *-e-*.

F. Rhyme Types

In general, rhyme involves the repetition of a terminal sound, but this must be defined conventionally.

F.1. Rich, Sufficient, Poor

Most histories of French verse acknowledge a hierarchy of rhyme types involving increasingly complex rhymes. In its basic form, the minimally accepted rhyme is called a *sufficient* rhyme. This generally is defined as a terminal tonic vowel and preceding consonant. Anything less than a sufficient rhyme (say, a rhyme involving a consonant and unaccented vowel, or a rhyme involving only the terminal tonic vowel) is classified as *poor.* A *rich* rhyme might be defined as one involving more than what is required for a sufficient rhyme. A simplified definition of this hierarchy is: one homophone—poor rhyme; two homophones—sufficient rhyme; three homophones—rich rhyme.

F.1.1. Rich rhyme is conventionally obligatory when sufficient rhyme is formed by endings of frequent occurrence, for example, *-ue, -er(s),* or for words ending in such endings as *-eux* or *-eur.* In cases where one of the words in such a rhyme pair is monosyllabic, the rhyme is generally acceptable and considered sufficient: *humeur/peur.* Examples of various rhyme types in Baudelaire's "Au lecteur": sufficient rhymes: *lices/vices; cris/débris;* rich rhyme: *immonde/le monde.*

F.1.2. Rhymes that are more complex than this would be called "over-curious" (so DuBellay), or sometimes "leonine" (the term is also used of internal rhymes in the first hemistich of an Alexandrine). *Ménades/sérénades* from Hugo's "Navarin" is an example.

F.2. Acceptable Rhyme Types

A rhyme is determined in part grammatically, in part by ear, and in part by convention.

F.2.1. A short vowel cannot be rhymed with a long vowel; but the first person future of a verb ending in *-er* (*-ai*) can rhyme with *-é;* and some diphthongs can rhyme with simple elements: *livre/suivre.* Words that have different syllable counts due to technicalities of verse rules can also rhyme, e.g., *biens/liens* (see sec. A.3.2.1 above; *biens,* from Latin *bene,* is monosyllabic; *liens,* from Latin *ligare,* is disyllabic).

F.2.2. Examples include *parole/folle* or *sain/tien.* Terminal *-s, -z,* and *-x* are considered equivalent. The acceptability of such rhymes in early verse depends on whether they are pronounced the same in *liaison,* that is, when followed by a word with an initial vowel. Thus *nous/loups* is acceptable; *nous/loup* is not (see Kastner, pp. 41–43).

F.3. Examples

Examples of the above rhyme types can be found in any classical or romantic French poem. Malherbe, "Dessein de quitter une dame": *incertaine/peine; plus je prise/ma prise* (same sound, different grammatical function); *l'effet/défait.* Baudelaire, "Au lecteur": *corps/remords; lâches/taches; serpents/rampants; involontaire/mon frère.*

F.4. Basic Rhyme Pairs

The basic patterns of rhyme pairs are *rhymes plates* (aabb), *rhymes croisés* (abab), and *rhymes emboités* (abba). These are familiar to any English reader of sonnets, where the rhymes of quatrains show all three forms.

F.4.1. In such rhyme pairs, most French verse requires the alternation of masculine rhymes (with a terminal tonic accent) and feminine rhymes (with a post-tonic element).

G. Fixed Forms

The *formes fixes* were a staple of earlier manuals on versification but receive less emphasis in recent ones. They are in origin medieval musical forms. Forms of the *rondeau* appear in various genres, including late-medieval religious plays. French fixed forms were revived in the late nineteenth century, both in France and in England, and curiously, many of the revived English variants are more rigid than the French. Some of the more important fixed forms are given below.

G.1. Sonnet

French sonnets are in fourteen lines, generally Alexandrines. The major French form has two quatrains (abba or abab) followed by two three-line stanzas (these can be rhymed variously: cdc dee, cdd cee, ccd ede, etc.)

G.2. *Ballade*

The late medieval form of the *ballade* found in the work of Deschamps consists of three eight-line stanzas in decasyllables, rhymed ababbcbc, followed by a shorter envoy. Villon's "Ballade des pendus" is in ten-line stanzas with a five-line envoy. The "Ballade de Villon a s'amye" (with his name in acrostics) is in eight-line stanzas. Examples of the *ballade* also occur in octosyllables.

G.3. *Rondeau*

A *rondeau* involves the repetition of a two-line refrain. The basic medieval form is as follows (the refrain is represented with AB, rhymes in a and b):

A	*Quant j'ay ouy le tabourin*
B	*Sonner pour s'en aler au may*
b	En mon lit fait n'en ay effray
a	Ne levé mon chef du coissin
a	En disant: "Il est trop matin
b	Ung peu je me rendormiray,"
A	*Quant j'ay ouy le tabourin*
a	Jeunes gens partent leur butin!
b	De Nonchaloir m'acointeray,
b	A lui je m'abutineray:
a	Trouvé l'ay plus prochain voisin,
A	*Quant j'ay ouy le tabourin*
B	*Sonner pour s'en aler au may.*

(Charles d'Orleans)

[When I hear the drum / sound to rise in May, / In my bed, I am not afraid, / nor do I raise my head from the pillow, / Saying: It is too early; / I will doze a bit more, / when I hear the drum. / Young people share their booty! / I know Indifference. / I will share with him. / I have found him my nearest neighbor. / When I hear the drum / sound to rise in May.]

G.3.1. Among many variants is the *rondeau redoublé,* whereby each of the four lines in the opening stanza is repeated as a refrain in the four following stanzas (a modern version is Theodore de Banville's "Rondeau Recoublé, à Silvie").

G.4. *Virelai*

Unlike the sonnet (sec. G.1 above) and the villanelle (sec. G.5 below), the *virelai* was not revived after the Middle Ages. It is a poem consisting of two or three stanzas of what is called the *bergerette,* a form of the *rondeau,* with the refrain repeated in its entirety. The *virelai* begins with a refrain of several lines, and this refrain closes each stanza. The abstract form is as follows:

Refrain (A)
Stanza I: B (B1 and B2)
        C (C1 and C2 [C2 = A])
Stanza II: B
        C

The following example is from Deschamps, "Virelay":

Dame, je vous remercy
et gracy
de cuer, de corps, de pensee
de l'anvoy qui tant m'agree } A
que je dy
c'onques plus biau don ne vi
faire a creature nee

plus plaisant ne plus joly,
ne qui sy } B1
m'ait ma leesce doublee;

Car du tout m'a assevi
et ravi   } B2
en l'amoureuse contree

je le porte avecques my
con cellui
qui m'a joye recouvree,
et si m'a renouvellee   } C1
m'amour, qui
m'auroit par rapporz häy
et par fausse renommee

Dame, je vous remercy
et gracy
de cuer, de corps, de pensee
de l'anvoy qui tant m'agree   } C2 (= A)
que je dy
c'onques plus biau don ne vi
faire a creature nee

G.5. Villanelle

The medieval *villanelle* enjoyed a resurgence in the nineteenth century and assumed a more rigid form, particularly and strangely among English writers. In its strictest form, it is nineteen lines of three-line units, with an intercalated, two-line rhyming refrain (represented in the following schema by A1 and A2, in italics). Among many English versions is Dylan Thomas's "Do Not Go Gentle into That Good Night."

A1 *Do not go gentle into that good night;*
b   Old age should burn and rave at close of day;
A2 *Rage, rage against the dying of the light.*

a   Though wise men at their end know dark is right,
b   Because their words had forked no lightning they
A1 *Do not go gentle into that good night.*

a   Good men, the last wave by, crying how bright
b   Their frail deeds might have danced in a green bay,
A2 *Rage, rage against the dying of the light.*

a   Wild men who caught and sang the sun in flight,
b   And learn, too late, they grieved it on its way,
A1   *Do not go gentle into that good night.*

a   Grave men, near death, who see with blinding sight
b   Blind eyes could blaze like meteors and be gay,
A2   *Rage, rage against the dying of the light.*

a   And you, my father, there on the sad height,
b   Curse, bless, me now with your fierce tears, I pray.
A1   *Do not go gentle into that good night.*
A2   *Rage, rage against the dying of the light.*

Note that the syntax of the refrain changes, although the sound and orthography do not.

Texts: Text of Baudelaire is from Oxford World's Classics, Oxford Univ. Press, 1993; early medieval works from Karl Bartsch, *Chrestomathie de l'ancien français (viiie–xve siècles)* (1866; 12th ed., New York: Hafner, 1951). Modern French examples are from Pléiade editions: *Anthologie de la poésie française (Moyen Age, xvie siècle, xvie siècle)*; and *Anthologie de la poésie française (xviie siècle, xixe siècle, xxe siècle)* (Paris: Gallimard, 2000); all translations are mine.

References: Benoît de Cornulier, *Art poëtique: notions et problèmes de métrique* (Lyons: Presses Universitaires de Lyon, 1995); W. Theodor Elwert, *Traité de versification française des origines à nos jours* (Paris: Klincksieck, 1965; trans. of *Französische Metrik*, 1961); L. E. Kastner, *A History of French Versification* (Oxford: Clarendon Press, 1903); Georges Lote, *Histoire du vers français*, 3 vols. (Paris: Boivin, 1949); Jean Mazaleyrat, *Elements de métrique française* (Paris: Armand-Colin, 1974); Warner Forrest Patterson, *Three Centuries of French Poetic Theory: A Critical History of the Chief Arts of Poetry in France (1328–1630)* (Ann Arbor: Univ. of Michigan Press, 1935); Clive Scott, *French Verse-art: A Study* (Cambridge: Cambridge Univ. Press, 1980).

Chapter Four

Accentual Verse

Old English

A. *Basic Linguistic Principles*
B. *Standard Descriptions of Verse*
C. *Musical Notation*
D. *Germanic Variants*

The third system of versification we will deal with is accentual verse, also known as "tonic" verse. As is the case with isosyllabic verse, little if any historical verse is purely accentual: all European verse described as accentual has basic or secondary rules regarding syllable number or even syllable length. Thus the standard distinction between English verse as "accentual-syllabic" and early Germanic verse as "accentual" is misleading. I take as a model Old English verse (700–1100). The principles outlined here can be applied to other early Germanic verse such as Old Norse; later forms of medieval Germanic verse including Middle English verse show only traces of these early systems.[1]

A. Basic Linguistic Principles

Most scholars agree on the basic constitutive elements of early Germanic verse:

---

1. Note on special characters: ð and þ are alternate ways of representing *th;* æ is a simple vowel, not a diphthong, and it can be long or short. Some transcriptions distinguish pure vowels from open variants with a cedilla, but that distinction has no bearing on meter and is not made here. 3 (yogh) is a special consonant representing several sounds in Old English; it can be conventionally transcribed as the letter *g.*

a) *syllable count and syllable length*
b) *word accent*
c) *alliteration*

A.1. Vowel and Syllable Length

As in Latin, syllables in Old English are distinguished linguistically as long or short in quantity. A syllable is considered long *metrically* if (1) it contains a naturally long vowel, or (2) it is followed by particular consonant combinations. Also as in Latin, the combination of a short, accented syllable followed by a second syllable can be considered a resolved long; that is, it is metrically equivalent to one long syllable. Vowel quantities can be determined etymologically; and in some cases they can be determined, through somewhat circular reasoning, by the use of such vowels in poetry.

A.1.1. Modern dictionaries and editions of Old English generally mark long vowels. Old English manuscripts themselves, however, do not, and recent editorial and scholarly transcriptions have tended to follow this practice. I mark them in my transcriptions here, although the meter of Old English is perfectly intelligible without knowledge of these vowel quantities.

A.1.2. Diphthongs

Old English diphthongs, like single vowels, are also distinguished linguistically as long or short. Among the more common diphthongs are *eo, ea,* and *ie.* The conventional way of marking a long diphthong in modern transcriptions is with a macron over the first element. Thus in the word *fēond, ēo* is a long diphthong in a single, metrically long syllable. In *heofon, eo* is a short diphthong, and the syllable in which it appears is metrically short.

A.2. Accent

Germanic word accent is "regressive"—that is, it has moved backward from its position in proto-Germanic, the hypothesized ancestor of modern Germanic languages. In all recorded Germanic languages, this accent falls on the root syllable (the first syllable of a word unless the first syllable is a common prefix). Thus, in the following passage from "The Wanderer," multisyllabic words have their accent on the first syllable: SIG-on; SUM-e; AN-geald, etc. The root syllable of ge-LAMP is the second syllable:

sigon þā to slǣpe. Sume sāre angeald
ǣfonrǣste, swā him ful oft gelamp.

Prefixes that do not receive a word accent in multisyllabic words
are easily recognized, often simply by their modern English cog-
nates. For example, *bi-dǣled;* other examples of words with common,
unaccented prefixes are *ge-bīdeð, ge-myndig, ā-secgan* (all from "The
Wanderer").

A.2.1. Compound Words

Many early Germanic words are compounds, that is, single words
formed of combinations of substantives: noun/noun, adjective/
noun, noun/gerund, etc. Compound words formed of independent
word elements have a primary accent on the root syllable of the first
word element; the second word element retains its accent as a secondary accent: the compound word *lagu-lāde* (sea-way) thus has a primary accent on *la-* in *lagu,* and a secondary accent on the first syllable of *-lāde.* Other examples from "The Wanderer" are *mōd-cearig,*
mōd-sefan, ferð-locan (which I will somewhat desperately translate as
"spirit-caring," "spirit-heart," and "spirit-locker"). The secondary accent can partake of the metrical structure of some half-lines; in others, it is apparently disregarded.

A.3. Alliteration

Germanic verse is organized in large part by *alliteration,* that is, the
repetition of the first stressed consonant or vowel sound in a word.
The importance of such alliteration is clearly related to the regressive nature of the Germanic word accent, although both the development of Germanic verse and the movement of the accent occurred
before written records exist. The alliterating element in a compound
word is always on the root syllable of the first word element. These
alliterations are generally evident in the transcription of any early
Germanic line:

Warað hine wrǣclāst,   nales wunden gold,
ferðloca frēorig,   nalǣs foldan blǣd.
("The Wanderer")

In these lines, the alliteration is on *w* in line 1 and *f* in line 2.

A.3.1. A curious feature of early Germanic verse is that all initial vowels are considered metrically acceptable alliterations. This is likely due to the fact that in the earliest Germanic verse each word root consisted of the form CVC (consonant-vowel-consonant). Words with initial vowel are the result of the loss of a consonant in proto-Germanic. These words traditionally alliterated with that consonant and continued to do so after it was lost. Thus, in "The Wanderer," line 8:

> Oft ic sceolde āna   uhtna gehwylce

The alliterating words are *āna,* and *uhtna,* and likely *Oft.*

A.3.2. Consonant Combinations
In general, alliterations involve only a single consonant; *w-* alliterates with *w-, wl-,* and *wr-; d-* with *d-* and *dr-,* etc. Poems occasionally give apparent (but illusory) evidence that more than the initial element is involved (e.g., *hr-* in "The Seafarer," line 32, and "The Wanderer," line 77, cf. line 72). Exceptional is the consonant *s: st-* alliterates only with *st-; sc-* only with *sc-;* and *s-* only with *s + vowel* or *s + -n-* ("The Wanderer," lines 93, 101).

B. Standard Descriptions of Verse
Standard descriptions of Latin and French verse are based on the theories and terminology of contemporary or near-contemporary writers for whom these were living languages. Early Germanic languages, by contrast, were not living languages for those who developed what are now the standard descriptions of its verse; the earliest description of Icelandic verse is by the thirteenth-century saga writer and historian Snorri Sturluson, who admits that the earlier poets may not have followed his prescriptions. Old English poems were unknown to English readers until the late sixteenth century; *Beowulf* was unknown until the late eighteenth century. Scholarship on Old English verse begins in the seventeenth century; it is thus historical and largely descriptive. My account below is based on what became the standard description of this verse in the late nineteenth and early twentieth centuries.

B.1. Basic Line Structure
Manuscripts of Old English do not represent verse line structure by writing on successive lines. The only indication of lines and half-lines

are raised dots between these units. In some of the earliest printed editions of Old English verses from the nineteenth century, the line unit is the half-line; in twentieth-century transcriptions, the basic line unit that is represented typographically is the complete line, consisting of two half-lines with a space between them.

B.1.1. Old English verse is constructed in pairs of half-lines joined by alliteration. A normal half-line contains two prominent accented syllables; the potentially alliterating elements are the initial consonants or vowels of these accented syllables. These accented syllables must contain a long syllable or the equivalent of a long syllable. In the second half-line, the first principal accent must partake in the line's alliteration. In the first half-line, either or both of the accented syllables must alliterate.[2]

$$\overset{\prime}{} \quad\quad \text{x x} \mid \overset{\prime}{} \ \text{x x} \quad\quad \overset{\prime}{} \ \text{x x x} \mid \overset{\prime}{} \ \text{x}$$

healdne his hordcofan,   hycge swā he wille

("The Wanderer")

B.1.2. Alliterating elements must be the principal word elements in any half-line, that is, nouns, adjectives, principal verbs, and stressed adverbs. Prepositions, pronouns, and auxiliary verbs are metrically unstressed.

B.1.3. The words *arsis* and *thesis* are unavoidable here: in descriptions by late-nineteenth-century German philologists, each half-line consists of two feet, measures, or metra. In each foot, the accented, alliterating element is the arsis (*Hebung*, translated variously as "lift" or "rise"); the unaccented elements form the thesis (*Senkung*, "sinking," or "dip").[3] In the second foot of the first half-line above, the arsis is *hord-;* the thesis is *-cofan.* For certain common line types, these terms

---

2. For my modifications of this conventional system of notation, see sec. B.2.1 below.

3. The German words are unambiguous, although the classical terms they translate (*arsis* and *thesis*) are not (see chap. 2, B.3.2 and note 3). For German, the late-Latin use of the terms is more convenient; the *Hebung* (= arsis) corresponds roughly to the verse accent (*ictus*) in classical verse.

pose no difficulty: the above line shows two half-lines, each with two easily recognized "stresses" or "lifts" (arses) and two corresponding "dips" or unstressed elements (theses); these form two feet. But not all half-line types consist of symmetrical measures or feet.

B.2. Eduard Sievers's System

The most important attempt to categorize Germanic verse types was by Eduard Sievers in the late nineteenth century. Sievers's system is purely descriptive and taxonomic. It distinguishes half-line types by certain rhythmic patterns. It does not imply that these half-line types are foundational; that is, they do not generate verse types nor were they known and consciously deployed by the poets themselves. Even scholars who reject Sievers's terminology assume their readers understand the basic components of this system.

B.2.1. Half-line Types

There are five basic half-line types in Sievers's system, labelled A–E. Each verse or half-line consists of two feet or metra, and the units that make up a foot are called *Glieder* (sing. *Glied,* "member" or "limb"). Basic half-line types have four *Glieder.* The basic A-type verse or half-line has, in Sievers's system, two feet of two *Glieder.* Many transcriptions of Sievers's system use a form of the notation shown in section B.1.1 above, whereby accented elements are marked with an acute accent (´), secondary accents are marked with a grave accent (`), and unaccented syllables are marked with an x. This form of notation is useful in analyzing individual lines. But to show basic patterns, I have modified it slightly, and in my representation below, X represents an accented long syllable or its equivalent; x represents a variable number of unaccented syllables; S represents a syllable with a secondary accent. In the simplest line, each *Glied* is equivalent to a syllable; but for most lines, the unstressed element (x) consists of more than one syllable. What are conventionally regarded as Sievers's five types of half-lines are as follows:[4]

---

4. Although Sievers does define two D-type half-lines in this fashion, his own numbering and classification of D-lines differs from the conventional representation I reproduce here; see *Altgermanische Metrik,* pp. 31 and 34.

A-type: X x | X x
B-type: x X | x X
C-type: x X | X x
D-type:
        D1   X | X S x
        D2   X | X x S
E-type: X S x | X

In D and E types, the vertical line represents a word break (or the break between the word elements of a compound word) and a hypothesized foot break. In D-type half-lines, the first foot contains a single accented syllable or its equivalent; in E-type half-lines, the final foot consists of a single accented syllable. Thus, for D1: *fold-buenda; wadan wræclastas.* D2-type half-lines have a terminal accent and often consist of three words (e.g., *eald enta geweorc*). E-type half-lines end in an accented monosyllable but are otherwise formally close to D2 types: XS(x) X: *orhfulne sīð; ginfæste gife; blædfastne beorn* (these examples from *Beowulf*). The opening lines of "The Wanderer" are as follows:

Oft him ānhaga	āre gebīdeð	A (or C)	A
metudes miltse,	þēah þe hē mōdcearig	A	C
geond lagulāde	longe sceolde	C	A
hrēran mid hondum	hrimcealde sæ,	A	E
wadan wraeclastas;	wyrd bið ful ārǣd	D1	A

B.2.1.1. Some verse types are complicated by a feature called *anacrusis,* or extra-metrical syllables preceding the half-line type. Thus, an A-verse can take the form x | X x | X x: *gecunnod on cēole* (*Beowulf,* line 5).

B.2.2. Hypermetric Lines
In addition to the regular lines described above, Old English verse contains what are called hypermetric lines. These lines are longer than the lines defined in Sievers's system and are perhaps expansions of them through the addition of an extra metron. They appear often in religious verse ("The Dream of the Rood"; "Judith") and in what are called the gnomic sections of more traditional verse, such as in "The Seafarer," or as here, in "The Wanderer":

Swā cwæð snottor on mōde,   gesæt him sundor æt rūne.
Til bið sē þe his trēowe gehealdeð: ne sceal næfre his
    torn tō rycene
beorn of his brēostum ācæþan

[Thus the wise man spoke in his mind; he sat apart in thought. Blessed be the man who keeps his pledges; nor is too quick to make his anger known]

Hypermetric lines can be seen as variants of Sievers's half-line types; in the second line above, introductory phrases are added to the basic alliterating half-lines: *trēowe gehealdeð* and *torn tō rycene* (both of type A).

B.3. Critiques of Sievers

Sievers's system has been much criticized. His verse types are not evenly distributed, and there seems to be no rationale in his analysis to explain, say, the rarity of B half-lines, or to deny theoretical combinations such as X x x X, combinations that do occur in modern versions of these lines (for example, in Ezra Pound's translation of "The Seafarer").

B.3.1. In *The Meter and Melody of Beowulf* (1974), Thomas Cable addresses some of these issues by considering Sievers's half-line types in terms of rising or falling stress, that is, the relative stress between adjoining elements. Cable hypothesizes a rule whereby, in adjoining stressed elements, the second element always receives a lesser stress; but half-lines with adjoining unstressed *Glieder* are forbidden. Cable's representation of Sievers's system is as follows:

A: $1 \backslash 2 / 3 \backslash 4$
B: $1 / 2 \backslash 3 / 4$
C: $1 / 2 \backslash 3 \backslash 4$
D1: $1 \backslash 2 \backslash 3 \backslash 4$
D2/E: $1 \backslash 2 \backslash 3 / 4$

Cable's rule thus allows for only five forms that are mathematically possible by simply combining stressed and unstressed *Glieder,* and these are in fact the five forms that appear in actual Old English verse.

B.3.2. Whereas Cable retains Sievers's types as a framework, other scholars, such as Geoffrey Russom, do away with Sievers's system altogether, criticizing it for failing to deal with basic issues of syntax and word structure. In *Old English Meter and Linguistic Theory* (1987), Russom reconceptualizes the minimal units of half-line structure, which are no longer formal and abstract (units that look like classical iambs or trochees). What Russom calls "foot patterns" are constructed of three basic linguistic elements: x is an unstressed element; S a fully stressed element; s of secondary stress. Acceptable foot patterns include many familiar from Sievers (Sx: *dryhten;* Ss: *saemann*). But many of Sievers's basic feet (xS) Russom rejects. In Russom's notation, Sievers's B half-lines are analyzed x/Sxs or x/Sxxs; C half-lines as x/Sxx or x/Ssx, with foot breaks corresponding to word breaks.

C. Musical Notation
C.1. Andreas Heusler
In his *Deutsche Versgeschichte* (1925–29), Andreas Heusler criticizes Sievers's system as mere "Augenphilology" (philology for the eye), arguing instead for a rhythm-based system based on musical measures (*Takte*). This system was developed by H. Möller in the nineteenth century and much criticized by Sievers himself. In Heusler's transcription, each half-line has a "ground-form" of two measures of quarter notes in 4/4 time, with possible extra-metrical elements preceding them. Heusler represents this ground-form as follows:

.. | x x x x | x x x x

In each measure, there are two beats: a full stress on the first element, and a secondary stress on the third. A standard A-verse (e.g., *gomban gyldan*) would be analyzed as two measures, each consisting of an accented half note, a quarter note, and a quarter rest. The deployment of rests and Heusler's use of four types of accents (single and double forms of acute and grave) become more complex with other line types (examples from Caedmon's hymn in Heusler, 1:143–44; Heusler's explanation, 1:33–34).

C.2. J. C. Pope

In *The Rhythm of Beowulf* (1942), J. C. Pope took this musically based theory further, translating Heusler's often eccentric notation back into musical notation and exploiting the idea that Old English verse was accompanied by the harp. To Pope, the musical analogy is not metaphorical; Pope even criticizes Heusler's 4/4 tempo as too slow (a tempo Heusler chooses only for convenience) and instead uses 4/8 as the basic time signature.

C.2.1. In Pope's description, the harp alternates heavy and light strikes; each measure (half-line) has one primary strike of the harp and one secondary one, and the strike must always be on the first element of a measure. In A-type half-lines the heavy harp strikes coincide with the two main accents. But in B- and C-type half-lines, a harp strike precedes the initial unstressed elements; the arsis, or stressed element, of the first measure consists of a rest (no words) followed by an unstressed syllable or syllables forming the "dip," or thesis. Thus in my notation, B and C half-lines might be divided (as divided in Heusler and later in Russom) as follows:

B: . x | X x S
C: . x | X S x

Pope's musical analysis of such verses on pp. 164–65 is as follows:

B-verse: *syððan ǣrest wearð* (*Beowulf*, line 6)

C-verse: *ofer hronrāde* (*Beowulf*, line 10)

In these scansions, as in Heusler's, the verse accent (ictus) is not represented in the written words themselves; furthermore, Pope's scansions disregard syllable length, which would seem essential to any description that involves musical notation.

C.3. Limitations

The hypotheses of Pope and Heusler are compelling, but they may have little to do with Old English verse composition. We have no idea how Old English verse was composed apart from the mythical story in Bede regarding the illiterate poet Caedmon (where there is no mention of a harp) and little specific evidence of how it was performed other than allusions to the harp accompaniment in poems such as *Beowulf.* The descriptions by Heusler and Pope work because they use a flexible system of notation—classical musical notation—one that has proven to be useful in describing music much different from that which it was originally meant to describe. German philologists often used this terminology metaphorically. Pope seems to literalize it, and even uses his own contemporary performance (see pp. 38–39) as evidence not only of the relation between half-lines but of the actual historical method of performance that underlies the text.

D. Germanic Variants

D.1. Old Norse and Old Saxon

The earliest Germanic poetry contemporary with Old English can be analyzed according to Sievers's system.

D.1.1. Old-Saxon *Heliand* (ninth century):

Than uuârun thoh sia fiori te thiu	
under thera menigo, | thia habdon maht godes,	C | C
helpa fan himila, | hêligna gêst	A | A
craft fan Criste.	A

D.1.2. The following Old Norse selection is nearly contemporary:

Ek man iotna,	ár um borna,	A | A
thá er forthom mik	foedda hoftho;	B | A
nío man ek heima,	nîo îvithi	A | D
miotvith maeran	fyr mold nethan	A | C

Later Old Norse poetry (Skaldic poetry) develops other more elaborate verse forms that will not concern us here.

D.2. Later Medieval German Variants

D.2.1. Later Germanic verse, particularly when it includes the same thematic material found in Old Norse verse, incorporates at least some of the principles of earlier Germanic verse. The following from the twelfth-century *Nibelungenlied* is written in four-line rhymed stanzas:

> Es wuohs in Búrgónden   ein vil édel magedin,
> daz in allen landen   nicht schoeners mochte sîn,
> Kriemhilt geheizen: si wart ein scoene wîp
> dar umbe muosen degene   vil verlîesén den lîp

The stanza consists of four lines formed of two half-lines, conventionally called the a-verse and b-verse. B-verses show masculine end-rhymes in the pattern aabb. A-verses show feminine rhymes in the same pattern. Standard accounts in literary histories describe these half-lines as accentual. Each half-line consists of three "lifts"; the final half-line (4b) consists of four "lifts." (In Heusler's account, each is a modification of a four-stress "ground-form.") If this account is accurate, stresses may be rhetorical rather than linguistic; they are determined not by the particular meaning of a line but rather by how that meaning might be expressed in performance. Exactly where such stresses are to be placed may not be always obvious to non-native speakers of Old High German.

D.2.2. By contrast, Gottfried von Strassburg's *Tristan* (twelfth century) clearly imitates the octosyllabic verse used in French chivalric romances and can be usefully described in the terms familiar to most English speakers: here iambic tetrameter—four feet of iambs, defined by stress—x ´ x ´ x ´ x ´:

> Gedaht man in ze guote niht
> von den der werlde guot geschicht
> so ware ez allez alse niht,
> swaz guotes in der werlt geschicht.

There is in this no trace of the earlier Germanic verse seen in the earliest Old Norse poems or in Old English poetry.

D.3. Middle English

D.3.1. The twelfth-century "The Owl and the Nightingale," in rhymed couplets, may well be analyzable in what has become the standard language used for discussing English verse, that is, in terms of units of feet. It is the first Middle English poem written out in lines rather than as continuous prose in its manuscript:

> Ich wes in one sumere dale
> In one swithe dẏele hale
> Iherde ich holde grete tale
> An vle and one nyhtegale.

D.3.2. In other early lyric verse, some remnant of alliteration is found but seems to have become more decorative than structural. The metrical basis of the following verse from the thirteenth-century Harley Manuscript 2253 is far from obvious:

> Lenten ys come wiþ love to toune,
> Wiþ blosmen & wiþ briddes roune,
>   þat al þis blisse bryngeþ;
> Dayes-eȝes in þis dales,
> Notes suete of nyhtegales,
>   Vch foul song singeþ.

These are perhaps octosyllables. Or should we describe these lines as having four required stresses where two must alliterate? Is this the combination of two or more distinct metrical systems, for example, accentual-alliterative and rhyming? Or is one of these apparent systems purely secondary and ornamental?

D.3.3. Verse of the Alliterative Revival

The clearest analog to early Germanic verse occurs in the so-called alliterative revival of the fourteenth-century, for example, in William Langland's *Piers Plowman* and the poems of the *Pearl* manuscript. This verse, however, cannot be analyzed according to the principles used in early Germanic verse, and obviously, more than stress and alliteration is involved in its composition. Some poems incorporate elaborate rhyming stanzas (*Pearl*); for others, the rules for composition involve considerations of alliteration, syllable count, and accent. But the precise rules remain controversial, and only in extreme cases could one say a line fails to meet such rules. Although it is not obvious what the metrical rules for these lines might be, some of the general features of older Germanic verse apply:

> In a somer seson, whan softe was the sonne,
> I shoop me into shroudes as I a sheep were,
> In habite as an heremite unholy of werkes,
> Wente wide in this world wondres to here.
>
> (Langland, *Piers Plowman*)

The two half-lines are not equivalent, and the first half-line contains more alliteration than the second half-line. In addition, in these lines the metrical stresses are likely not the same as linguistic stresses, whatever the rules for their production might be.

D.4. Modern Variants

Remnants of early alliterative verse structure or allusions to it can be found in modern verse:

> Dem Schnee, dem Regen, dem Wind entgegen,
> Im Dampf der Klüfte, durch Nebeldüfte,
> Immer zu! immer zu! ohne Rast und Ruh.
> Lieber durch Leiden wollt ich mich schlagen,
> Als so viel Freuden des Lebens ertragen.
> Alle das Neigen von Herzen zu herzen,
> Ach, wie so eigen schaffet es Schmerzen
> Wie, soll ich fliehn? Wälderwärts ziehn?
> Alles, alles vergebens!
> Krone des Lebens, Glück ohne Ruh,
> Liebe bist du, o Liebe bist du.
>
> (Goethe, *Rastlose Liebe*
> [1815; transcription F. Schubert])

This verse by Goethe could be described in the classical language of feet and foot types. Yet classical foot-based metrics seems to fail here, just as surely as it does when confronting Hamlet's "To be or not to be." The Goethe poem follows or implies a musical form (as Schubert's musical setting, from which it is transcribed, suggests). But the half-line structure, alliteration, and stress patterns seem related as well to early Germanic verse types. There are numerous other variants in modern verse, most obviously, Gerard Manley Hopkins's sprung rhythm, which I discuss in chapter 6.

Texts: Old English texts from Frederic G. Cassidy and Richard N. Ringler, *Bright's Old English Grammar and Reader,* 3rd. ed. (New York: Holt, Rinehart and Winston, 1971) and Friedrich Klaeber, *Beowulf and the Fight at Finnsburg,* 3rd ed. (Lexington: D. C. Heath, 1950). Middle English texts adapted from O. F. Emerson, *A Middle English Reader* (New York: Macmillan, 1905) and Richard Morris and W. W. Skeat, *Specimens of Early English* (Oxford: Clarendon Press, 1873); early Germanic texts adapted from Friedrich v. der Leyen, *Deutsch Dichtung des Mittelalters* (Frankfurt-am-Main: Insel, 1962).

References: Thomas Cable, *The Meter and Melody of Beowulf* (Urbana: Univ. of Illinois Press, 1974); Andreas Heusler, *Deutsche Versgeschichte mit Einschluss des altenglischen und altnordischen Stabreimverses,* 3 vols. (Berlin: de Gruyter, 1925–29); Winfred P. Lehmann, *The Development of Germanic Verse Form* (Austin: Univ. of Texas Press, 1956); John Collins Pope, *The Rhythm of Beowulf: An Interpretation of the Normal and Hypermetric Verse-Forms in Old English Poetry* (New Haven: Yale Univ. Press, 1942) and "Old English Versification," in *Eight Old English Poems,* 3rd ed., ed. J. C. Pope, pp. 129–58 (New York: W. W. Norton, 2001); Geoffrey Russom, *Old English Meter and Linguistic Theory* (Cambridge: Cambridge Univ. Press, 1987); Eduard Sievers, *Altgermanische Metrik* (Halle: Niemeyer, 1893).

Chapter Five

The Power of Music

A. *Metaphors of Music and Metrics*
B. *Pseudo-Musical Forms*
C. *Wars of Words and Music*
D. *Blues: Text and Performance*
E. *Arbitrary Forms: Serial Music*

Music affects verse most directly when verse is constructed with a particular musical form as the constitutive element:

> One for the money,
> two for the show,
> three to make ready now go, cat, go.
> Now don't you step on my blue suede shoes.
> You can do anything but lay off of my blue suede shoes.

Various metrical systems could be imagined to explain these verses: syllabic, accentual, even quantitative. But just because a literary analysis can be made to work does not mean it is correct or even legitimate. The above lines are, as we all know, lyrics based on music, and that is how their metrical form must be analyzed. To know this of any given poem or lyric often requires external evidence: we own a recorded version of this song; our grandparents sang it to us. With historical verses, whether a musical basis exists often requires speculation based on what we can consider as evidence (see chap. 6, D on John Donne).

Such cases are individual: we must speak of particular poems and particular music. They provide, perhaps, a limit to what a general study of versification can tell us about certain verse. Yet the influence of music on verse and discussions of verse is often indirect and does not consist solely of these limiting cases.

A. Metaphors of Music and Metrics

This first section addresses the use of musical language and terminology in the critical discussion and description of verse. Words such as *rhythm, measure, tone, theme* are common in discussions of verse. For some musical terminology, the strain in its application to verse is obvious: the word *tone*, for example, was popularized by I. A. Richards early in the twentieth century as the attitude of poets toward their work. In this case, there seems no relation between a musical tone and whatever the word might mean in poetry, and it is possible that Richards himself did not intend the musical reference. Other musical terminology is more problematic: *motif* and *theme*, and technical words such as *measure, rhythm,* and *beat.* When applied to verse, are these literal? or are they purely metaphorical?

A.1. Musical Notation

Musical notation has been invoked in the description of many verse types, and we have discussed a particular case in chapter 4, C above. To describe verse in musical notation is not the same as to claim that verse has a musical basis. When a verse is written for music, the musical notation applies not to the words but to the music that the words happen to fit. It is thus not quite correct even in these cases to imagine that the words are a direct function of the musical notation. When musical notation is applied to verse without accompanying music, that language becomes metaphorical.

A.1.1. Quantitative dactyls in verse are often usefully described through classical Western musical notation as measures consisting of a stressed half note followed by two quarter notes in 4/4 time, or a quarter note followed by two eighth notes in 4/8 time. The two quarter notes can be exchanged with a half note (or the two eighth notes with a quarter note). The musical analogy fails, however, in describing other common feet: an anapest cannot conveniently be described as a measure of two quarter notes and one half note in

4/4 time, since the conventional stress in a Western musical measure is on the first beat; in an anapest, that stress (the *ictus*) is on the last.

A.1.2. Musical notation has other basic limitations when applied to verse. As noted by many linguists, the perceived distinction between long and short syllables, even in languages where this distinction is fundamental, is not quantifiable and cannot be reduced to a simple musical notation that suggests a short is exactly or approximately half the duration of a long. Even in verses where such substitution is permitted (Latin dactylic hexameter), that substitution is a matter of convention and not necessarily a product of acoustic or linguistic reality (two shorts equal a long by convention, not because they occupy the same amount of actual time). In verse without feet or in verse with more complex rules of substitution, the musical analogy is of no help. In the opening syllables of Aeolic verse, long and short syllables are equivalent (chap. 2, E); and in none of this verse is there anything that can be usefully described as analogous to a musical measure. Somewhat paradoxically, it is precisely this verse that has the most claim to a real musical foundation.

A.1.3. Finally, the history of Western musical notation is not parallel to the history of Western versification and at times diverges as well from the history of Western music itself. The fact that Western musical notation works so convincingly in the description of certain verse forms is not a sign of the musical basis of such verse but rather an indication of the flexibility of the language itself.

A.2. Technical Musical Terminology
A.2.1. The terms *measure, rhythm,* and *beat* are often applied to verse, without explicit musical notation. A measure in musical notation is a specific and definable unit that controls the basic, repeated rhythm of the piece. In 3/4 time, a measure is a group of three quarter notes or their equivalent with an implied accent (ictus) on the first. In 4/4 time, a measure consists of four quarter notes or their equivalent. The closest analogue in verse is the metron in classical iambic verse (see chap. 2, B.1.4). In French metrics, the term *measure* has been used to describe the phrasal units that make up an Alexandrine.

These units are not prescribed by rule but rather are the result of the particular phrase structure of particular lines; that is, a description of a French line in terms of such measures deals with the realized version of the verse pattern, not with the underlying structure. One line might have a structure 2 / 4 / 3 / 3; the following 1 / 5 / 4 / 2.

A.2.1.1. Such phrases are matters of stylistics and have nothing to do with the notion of a musical measure. A measure in music is a foundational unit (of description if not of composition); as used in the description of classical French Alexandrines (chap. 3, D.1), it is a unit that exists only in the analysis of particular verses. It is notable (perhaps the wrong word to use here!) that French music written during the period of the classical Alexandrine never treated its musical measures in this fashion.

A.2.2. The term *rhythm* can be particularly misleading in that it conflates levels of versification, composition, performance, stylistics, and even pure chance. The word is used in a number of senses but, to be intelligible, should refer to the deployment of variously marked elements in a line: in quantitative verse, it might be the relation of long and short syllables; in accentual verse, the relation of stressed and unstressed syllables. If these are basic elements of verse, rhythm is clearly part of versification, but if these are secondary elements, what we are dealing with is stylistics. In Greek or Latin hexameter, there is often a perceived rhythm of accents. But these accents can only be considered part of versification when there are specific rules or conventions for their use (for example, in Vergil's hexameters, word accent and ictus must correspond in the last two feet; see chap. 2, D.1.2). Other rhythmic patterns can also be defined. One could speak of a rhythm of accents, of long or short, or even particular sounds. The rhythm of line 1 of *Beowulf* might be different from the rhythm of line 2 in any of these senses. But this is not necessarily a matter of versification. Other cases may be purely illusory, for example, the rhythms of, say, the liquid consonants *r* and *l* in "Mary had a little lamb").

A.3. Motif and Theme
Musical terms on a higher level of organization include *motif* and *theme*. These are perfectly intelligible descriptive words for verse

if used in direct analogy with their meanings in music: a motif is a short, recognizable pattern of notes; a theme is a larger unit of musical elements. In music, however, these are generally not descriptive of basic features of composition, nor would they be in most conventional poetry.[1] Furthermore, the overuse of the word *theme* in literary criticism has rendered it almost useless for any purposes of literary analysis.

B. Pseudo-Musical Forms

Poets frequently allude to the real or imagined musical bases of their verse. In classical and modern verse, *sing* is conventionally used as a metaphor for the writing of poetry; *ode* derives from the Greek word for song; many poems use the refrain; and even pure verbal repetitions in some modern verse seem based on music. Some forms are direct products of music; others that adopt these forms as a convention effectively turn the musical foundation into a metaphor for musical foundation.

B.1. Pseudo-musical forms are often in fixed stanzaic form, many of which originated with medieval musical or dance forms, as their names sometimes suggest: *rondeau*, sonnet, *virelai*. The French "fixed forms" as defined in the nineteenth century are the clearest example; all originated in musical forms but in their revived form had little or nothing to do with music (see chap. 3, G).

B.1.1. The most common pseudo-musical form in English is the sonnet—a fourteen-line stanza composed of three quatrains and a concluding couplet (Shakespearean) or two quatrains followed by two tercets or three-line units (Petrarchan). The sonnet is in English a pure imitation, since the musical basis of the form was lost before the verse form was adopted in English. English writers copied what

---

1. A set of versification rules that incorporates motif and theme certainly could be devised. For example: A poem is in four lines. Line 1 must contain the word *lion;* line 2 must contain a statement concerning transcendental philosophy; line 3 must be in eight syllables.

was already a purely literary form from Petrarch, incorporating as they did some of the musical language that may or may not indicate the musical form.

B.2. Ode

One of the most interesting examples in English of a pseudo-musical form is the *ode*. Historically, the word has been used of two quite different genres, generally described as the Horatian ode and the English or romantic ode.

B.2.1. A Horatian ode is a variant of Horace's poems in Aeolic form (see chap. 2, E). Although Horace's meters could be imposed directly upon other languages, English versions usually only allude to that form. Classicists now disagree as to whether Horace's stanzas should be analyzed as three- or four-line stanzas, but editions of his poems have always printed them as four-line stanzas, and all imitations have used this form. Most versions of Horation ode also attempt to reproduce common themes in Horace. One of the most famous in English is Andrew Marvell's "An Horatian Ode: Upon Cromwell's Return from Ireland." The stanzaic form is shown in the following:

> The forward youth that would appear
> Must now forsake his Muses dear,
>   Nor in the shadows sing
>   His numbers languishing.

The relation to the Horatian ode is more visual than precisely metrical; Marvell's stanza is an apparent imitation of or allusion to the fifth Asclepiad (see chap. 2, E.3). The musical foundations of this form are remote and are little more than metaphorical even in Horace.

B.2.2. The second form of ode is the romantic or English ode, modelled after the Greek odes of Pindar. Most histories associate this genre with the mid-seventeenth-century poet Abraham Cowley, but the form appears earlier in Ben Jonson. Among the basic forms is a repeating three-stanza unit: in Jonson, these stanzas are labelled *turn, counter-turn,* and *stand* (translating *strophe, antistrophe, epode*). The antistrophe repeats the metrical form of the strophe; the epode has a new form. The following is the opening "Turne" of Jonson's "To the immortall memorie, and friendship of that noble paire, Sir Lucius Cary and Sir H. Morison":

> Brave Infant of Saguntum, cleare
> Thy coming forth in that great yeare,
> When the Prodigious Hannibal did crowne
> His rage, with razing your immortall Towne.
> Thou, looking then about,
> Ere thou were halfe got out,
> Wise child, didn'st hastily returne,
> And mad'st thy Mothers wombe thine urne.
> How summ'd a circle didst thou leave man-kind
> Of deepest lore, could we the Centre find!

B.2.2.1. English poets exploited both the obscurity of Pindar's language (as the above example shows) and the apparent freedom of Pindar's verse, a freedom perhaps enhanced by the obscurity of the fundamental rules of that verse. Many English odes, including those of Jonson, do not follow the three-stanza form but simply repeat a unique stanza. Since there was no set form in a Pindaric stanza, poets could use or invent any line or stanza in English, as long as the form was repeatable. Metrically coherent stanzas could be constructed of any length, in any meter or rhyme scheme (for example, in Coleridge's "Ode to Tranquillity"). In the fully developed romantic ode, even the requirement that successive stanzas repeat the same form is dropped (see as an example Coleridge's "Dejection: An Ode").

C. Wars of Words and Music

C.1. In 1602, Giulio Caccini published a book of madrigals, *Le Nuove Musiche,* with a polemical preface. In this preface, Caccini constructs a history of music casting himself and the members of his Florentine Camerata as reformers. The target of Caccini's polemic is the obscuring of words in traditional music. That words when sung were often unintelligible had been a theme in discussions of music for some time. In Dante's *Divine Comedy,* the obscurity of words is a given: "I seemed to hear a 'Te Deum' in voices mixed with melody. This image affected me just as when we hear people singing with an organ: now we understand the words, and now we do not" (Purgatory, canto 9). In its meetings of 1545–63, the Council of Trent had demanded that words in the Mass be intelligible: "For those masses celebrated with singing or with organ . . . the singing must be constituted so as not to give empty pleasure, but so that words can be clearly understood by all." And still today, lyrics of popular music are often ill-heard and misunderstood, or simply invented by individual listeners and amateur singers.

C.1.1. Caccini's polemic concerned secular music. To clarify the words, Caccini promotes monody over polyphony, that is, music with a single vocal line with harmonic accompaniment rather than the production of harmony through the combination of potentially independent melodic lines. The melody is itself subordinate to the words: notes are to be chosen, Caccini states, "according to the sentiments of the words."[2] In "The Role of the Guitar in the Rise of Monody" James Tyler notes that the popularity of the guitar is a direct function of this type of music.

C.1.2. The term Caccini used to describe the new style of music was *stilo rappresentativo*, generally translated as *recitative*, a declamatory verse set off from the more lyrical *aria*.[3] Music in this style, whether found in opera or madrigal writing, was to be entirely dependent on words, and no musical element (e.g., a melodic interval or musical rhythm) was to be constructed unless it accorded with the sen-

---

2. This history of early monody, and the centrality of the Florentine Camerata, was popularized by Giovanni Batista Doni in the mid-seventeenth century; Doni's discussion was itself published in the eighteenth century and popularized in English through Charles Burney's inclusion of it in his popular *General History of Music* in 1789. According to these histories, Italian opera as practiced in the eighteenth century originated in the theories of Caccini and his contemporaries and in the dominance of the word over music that they believed had precedent in the works of Plato. Caccini's preface is available in Strunk's *Source Readings in Music History*, pp. 607–17.

3. This became the basis for the distinction between recitative and aria in classical Italian opera; it is analogous to the difference between spoken and sung sections of eighteenth-century German *Singspiel* and even twentieth-century musical comedy.

timents expressed in the verse. Consequently, there was to be no purely virtuosic or ornamental musical element.

C.1.3. There are many paradoxes in this history. Caccini's theory legitimized a new style of verse, the recitative, in which ordinary principles and restrictions of versification and musical considerations did not apply. But in practice, Caccini's madrigals were innovative only in terms of music; many were written to support preexistent verse. Furthermore, the standard histories of opera beginning as early as the eighteenth century often complain that the style developed by Caccini and Monteverdi promoted the very kind of meaningless ornamented singing against which Caccini polemicized.

C.2. The History Revised

In the late nineteenth century, Nietzsche revisited the same polemic in *Birth of Tragedy*, with the operas of Richard Wagner as the central focus. In Nietzsche's revisionist version of this history, the villains were the Florentines themselves and the genre of modern opera, which Nietzsche attributes to them. In recitative, music is subordinate to words; in Nietzschean terms, the musical, Dionysian element is thus subordinated to the rational, Socratic element characteristic of decadent modern culture. Nietzsche promoted instead the dominance of music which, as an enthusiastic Wagnerian in these early writings, he claimed to find in certain passages of Wagner's *Tristan*.

C.2.1. Declamatory Verse

Wagner's early opera *Lohengrin* is written in large part in conventional rhyme pairs (*rhymes plates,* or *rhymes croisés*); these lines alternate with decasyllables with distinct iambic rhythm, imitating, it seems, conventional late-nineteenth-century descriptions of English blank verse. In Wagner's later work, an entirely different type of line develops. Some passages of what might be called musical highlights equivalent to the arias of the earlier operas are constructed on the basis of rhyme, accent, with a line length so short that these features appear to be ornamental rather than structural (e.g., the love-duet from *Tristan,* act 2, or the closing "Mild und leise" of act 3). Verses equivalent to earlier recitative seem roughly syllabic. In *The Ring*, declamatory verses often allude to verse systems and elements of verse systems (rhyme, meter, assonance, alliteration) but do not follow them. Even a visual inspection of the following lines from *Götterdämmerung*, act 3, reveals these allusions:

> Starke Scheite schichtet mir dort
> am Rande des Rheines zuhauf
> Hoch und hell lodre die Glut,
> die den edlen Leib
> des hehrsten Helden verzehrt. . . .
> Weiss ich nun, was dir frommt?
> Alles, alles, alles weiss ich,
> alles ward mir nun frei!
> Auch deine Raben höre ich rauschen;
> mit bang ersehnter Botschaft
> send' ich die beiden nun heim.
> Ruhe, ruhe, du Gott!

> ———

> [Stack stout logs for me in piles there / by the shore of
> the Rhine! High and bright let a fire blaze / which
> shall consume / the noble body of the mighty hero. . . .
> Everything, everything I know, / all is now clear to me! /
> I hear your ravens stirring too; / with dreaded desired
> tidings / I now send them both home. / Rest, rest now,
> o god!] (trans. Lionel Salter, Deutsche Grammaphone)

C.2.2. Such passages seem entirely freed of the constraints of versification, even while acknowledging and in some cases incorporating principles of those systems. In the language of the polemicists, the lines are constructed on the basis of the verbal meanings, not, as in classical verse, on abstract versification systems. Insofar as the music expresses both the specific and general content of these lines, the above example and others like it certainly seem in the spirit of Caccini's polemic, although Nietzsche claims otherwise, and Wagner himself was silent about these early polemics. Verse defined this way is perhaps conveniently not subject to ordinary formalist debate: one cannot provide evidence for why a particular verse might correctly or incorrectly represent the abstract idea it conveys or is meant to convey, nor could one expect any serious agreement on what that idea might be.

D. Blues: Text and Performance

One of the most significant forms of popular music produced in the twentieth century is blues. I include it here because most readers are familiar with it and because it shows the instability of the levels of composition and performance discussed throughout this study, as well as the difficulty of providing strict definitions for these levels. What are the differences between the underlying form (the meter and versification), the realization of that form in the composer's "text" or "song," the associated stylistic features of that realization, and the performed variations of that form and stylistic features?

D.1. Basic Blues Progression

The basic blues progression consists of three chords, in classical music theory known as the tonic, subdominant, and dominant (labelled I, IV, and V). For the key of E, these are E, A, and B; for the key of C, they are C, F, and G. Most beginning guitarists can learn these in a day or so and play tolerable blues accompaniment by the end of the week. What has come to be the typical blues progression is in the following form; each numeral is a measure of four beats and the entire progression is in twelve measures:

I (IV) I I
IV IV
I I
V IV I (V)

A familiar example is as follows:

| I | | (I/IV) | I | I |

      I   (I/IV)   I   I
I'm sitting here wondering will a matchbox hold my clothes
       IV   IV   I   I
I'm sitting here wondering will a matchbox hold my clothes
   V   IV
I ain't got no matches, but I still got a long way
  I   V
to go

There are thousands of blues songs written according to this formula.

D.2. Dropped Beat

A curious feature of these songs from a metrical standpoint can be seen by comparing some of the earliest recordings from the 1930s with recordings from the 1960s and later. Normally, one thinks of an evolving form as growing more complex and less rule-bound. In blues one hears the opposite. One of the most influential blues singers was Robert Johnson (d. 1938). Only twenty-nine songs in Johnson's original recordings still exist, a few of them in multiple versions and some released only in the 1960s. Most of these are in the repertoire of modern blues musicians. In these and in those of his contemporary Son House, one of the most striking characteristics is the "dropped beat." You can't tap your foot to the recording of Johnson's "I Believe I'll Dust My Broom"; if you do, you will quickly get lost. For Johnson, and for many other blues players, when the vocal line ended (say, in the first line above), and there was nothing of any particular interest happening on the guitar, it was perfectly appropriate simply to begin the next line, cutting out part of the final measure of I. If too much was happening on the guitar, or the guitarist had difficulty negotiating a passage, the final bar could be extended.

The dropped beat (or less commonly an added beat) is so conventional in early blues that it is almost a rule.[4] Even performances that are technically in perfect rhythm incorporate the illusion of such a missed beat (of many examples, the recording by Son House of "Lay Down Dirty Blues"). One could argue that the dropped beat is a conventional sign of spontaneity, in the same way as are the often bizarre and incongruous lyrics of a song such as Johnson's "Red Hot." This feature is often imitated in mid-century folk music, in much jazz, but oddly, rarely heard in standard blues of the late twentieth century. A performer such as B. B. King never in any of the recordings I've heard drops or adds a beat.

D.2.1. Implications

So let us suppose, hypothetically, that this dropped beat marks the difference between '20s blues singers and those from the '70s and

---

4. This is also a characteristic feature of much of the early music collected in *American Primitive: Vol. II: Pre-War Revenants (1897–1939)*, collected by John Fahey, Revenant Records, RVN 214, 2005.

'80s. How do we describe it? One can define various levels here; for convenience, I will define four, but curious readers can of course multiply these: the abstract rigid form, the form realized in a particular song (by a composer), the song realized in a particular performance (by a performer), what is heard or experienced by a listener. The composer is certainly aware of each level, as is the listener listening to or imagining any particular song or performance.

It is tempting to try to arrange these levels in a hierarchy, but no hierarchy seems to work. I simply pose the alternatives below:

a) *The dropped beat is simply a matter of performance;* it is not imagined by the composer, and the listener experiences it simply as a quirk of a performer.

b) *The dropped beat is part of the form itself, as much a requirement for early blues as the progression itself.* Thus the written form of the song (in, say, classical Western musical notation) falsifies the actual song, however we define what that actual song might be.

c) *The dropped beat is ignored by the listener.*

d) *The dropped beat is purely a function of musical competence:* an amateur or professional musician working on or performing a song can add or drop beats at will. These are of absolutely no consequence unless an uninvited listener walks into the room.

e) *The dropped beat is purely a matter of considerations of performance:* soloists rarely get lost or tangled in strange rhythms and can always find or define their way out of such entanglements; a group, by contrast, needs a clearer rhythmic pattern in order to play together in a coherent fashion (jazz musicians of course might dispute this).

D.3. There is no need to confine this discussion to blues; the performed quirks of country music and folk music (deliberate vocal breaks, bad intonation, etc.) are analogous; and classical music poses the same problems from a somewhat different standpoint in the so-called original or period instrument revival and the surrounding polemics. The best a study of versification can do is pose a sketch of these levels, levels that may change in the history of a genre. In the above case, it is possible that stylistic quirks of Johnson become hardened into rules of performance, and finally into rules of genre. Or, alternatively, we could speak of a versification system as an abstract form realized most perfectly in a late, systematized form (perhaps the B. B. King version of the blues). Certain poetic cultures have a history congenial to this analysis (thus French verse evolves into a self-conscious classicism in the eighteenth century; quantitative verse evolves into the self-conscious and aristocratic Latin forms of the first century BCE). But for others, we must simply muck along as best we can.

E. Arbitrary Forms: Serial Music

Serial music or twelve-tone music is a particular form of what is called atonal music developed in the early twentieth-century by Arnold Schoenberg and Anton Webern. It is also the basis of the theories of music in Thomas Mann's *Doktor Faust*. I include it as an example of how art is liberated from traditional strictures, not simply by ignoring those strictures but rather by imposing new and even more radical strictures on it.

E.1. In its simplest form, serial music avoids all traditional harmonies and melodic conventions by imposing an entirely new set of rules. Essentially, the tonal elements are the twelve notes in an octave of a tempered keyboard, where each step is a half-tone: C, C#/Db, D, D#/Eb, E, F, F#/Gb, G . . . etc.

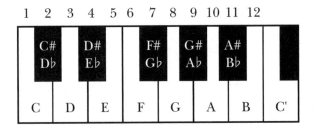

Each musical piece must be constructed of variants of a basic row of these twelve elements: the basic row consists of all twelve notes in whatever sequence the composer defines (say, 1, 9, 8, 6, 5, 3, 11, 10, 4, 2, 12, 7). I don't know what this sounds like, but I could find out by playing it on a piano (C, Ab, G, F . . .). This basic row can be varied by playing it as an *inversion*, whereby upward intervals become downward intervals (1 [=13], 5, 6, 8 . . .).[5] It can also be played back-ward (7, 12, 2, 4 . . .). It can also be played inverted and backward (7, 2, 12, 10 . . .). These four variant forms can then begin on any of the twelve notes themselves, giving forty-eight possible variations. Theoretically, there is no privileged note or apparent key in such music and no tonal center.

E.1.1. Modern listeners are familiar with much atonal music simply by being audiences of cinema. But most listeners not used to classical music will still find the sound of strict serial music as radical and jarring today as it was in the 1920s (listen, for example, to Webern's *Drei Geistliche Volkslieder* of 1925). Paradoxically for the modern ear the most radical of musics is that which was produced by the most systematic and rigorous application of rules.

E.2. Modern Verse Analogues
Twelve-tone music is analogous to the experiments conducted by such poets as Verlaine in the late nineteenth century and by many poets in the twentieth century. Although French poets wrote free verse and prose poems, some of the most disruptive and revolutionary writing by Verlaine was the result of his application of arbitrary but fixed rules for composition (see chap. 3, C.4.2). Examples are also easily found in pictorial art where some of the most visually unsettling works, such as the paintings of Uccello or the modern drawings of Henri Flocon, have been produced not by rejecting but by strictly following the rules and implications of linear perspective.

E.2.1. Self-conscious artificial procedures are also used notably by at least some of the L=A=N=G=U=A=G=E poets of the mid- and late twentieth century and in certain compositions (poetic and musical) by John Cage, where arbitrary rules and chance combine to produce

---

5. In an inversion, the successive note is found by inverting the interval between notes: if in the initial row, the next note is 5 half-steps higher than the first, in the inversion, that note will be 5 half-steps lower: one can produce these mechanically simply by subtracting the numbers in the series from some other number.

a work apparently free of strictures of traditional forms. It is often difficult to know whether the unsettling and often humorous effects produced by poets such as Susan Howe (e.g., from "The Midnight": "For here we are here / BEDHANGINGS . . .") or Ron Silliman ("I am Marion Delgado") are due to the complete absence of formal and thematic rules or to the rigid application of unimaginable ones.

Texts: Early English texts from facsimiles of original editions in Early English Books Online, eebo.chadwyck.com. Among the many blues compilations, see Robert Johnson, *Complete Recordings,* 2 discs, Sony, 1990.

References: Charles Burney, *A General History of Music: From the Earliest Ages to the Present Period,* 4 vols. (London, 1789; rpt. New York: Dover, 1935); Friedrich Nietzsche, *The Birth of Tragedy* (1872; trans. Walter Kaufman 1967; New York: Modern Library, 2000); W. Oliver Strunk, *Source Readings in Music History,* rev. ed., ed. Leo Treitler (New York: W.W. Norton, 1998); James Tyler, "Italy: The Role of the Guitar in the Rise of Monody," in James Tyler and Paul Sparks, *The Guitar and Its Music: From the Renaissance to the Classical Era,* pp. 37–50 (Oxford: Oxford Univ. Press, 2002). For the L=A=N=G=U=A=G=E poets, the evolving Wikipedia entry is perhaps the most appropriate starting point.

Chapter Six

Implications for the Study of English Verse

Four Studies

A. *English Versions of Quantitative Verse*
B. *Syllabic and Isosyllabic Verse Forms*
C. *Accentual Verse: Sprung Rhythm*
D. *Songs of John Donne*

A. English Versions of Quantitative Verse

The attempts of sixteenth- and seventeenth-century English poets to write verse according to the principles of quantity are well known, and several essays devoted to the topic were printed in the classic anthology of G. Gregory Smith, *Elizabethan Critical Essays* (1904). These efforts are generally dismissed as failures, as if there were something unnatural and perverse about the attempt to import foreign metrics into English or to force English to conform to non-English rules. But disparaging these attempts does little to clarify them. To introduce principles of quantity is no more or less disruptive of native English versification systems than to introduce versions of classical genres: comedy, tragedy, epic, etc.

A.1. Alternatives

There are three ways in which classical meters could be applied to English:

a) *Classical prosodic rules could be imposed directly.* English syllables would thus be defined as long or short the same way Latin syllables might be defined as long or short and verse forms written according to these quantities. Thus, the word *dying* would be scanned not as a trochee (´ x), that is, one stressed syllable followed by an unstressed syllable, but rather as a iamb (‿ _), that is, one short syllable followed by one long syllable.

b) *The distinction of long/short syllables in quantitative verse could be translated into a binary system of stress; that is, English stress would be the English prosodic equivalent of Latin quantity.* Thus, the English version of a Latin dactyl (_ ‿ ‿) would be ´ x x—one stressed syllable followed by two unstressed syllables; the word *dying* would be scanned as a trochee (one stressed syllable followed by an unstressed syllable). Longfellow's *Evangeline* is one of the most often cited examples of a poem written according to these principles.

´ x   x | ´ x   x | ´ x x | ´   x x | ´   x   x | ´ x

This is the forest primeval, the murmuring pines in the hemlock

c) *A presumably native English equivalent could be substituted for a classical verse type.* Milton thus writes *Paradise Lost* in what is known as blank verse, an English form that to Milton was analogous to the dactylic hexameter used in Homer and in Vergil, even though the two have little formal or prosodic relation.

A.2. Relation between Accentual and Quantitative Verse

For the modern reader and modern poet of English verse, foreign meter is interesting and useful insofar as it differs from what is thought to be ordinary English meter; a foreign (or arbitrary) verse system might thus be useful in freeing one of tradition (thus Marianne Moore's isosyllabic verse, or the work I note in chap. 5, E). Suppose one wished to revolutionize limerick writing and do away with the more constraining elements of tradition: one could write a limerick according to quantitative rather than accentual principles (see example, chap. 2, B.4, note 4). This would force the budding limerick writer to reimagine what constitutes a basic verse line. Imposing quantitative verse rules forces a writer into verbal constructions impossible under other systems, and it is the clash of the two systems that is most interesting.

Yet this was certainly not the intention of early modern writers such as Philip Sidney, Gabriel Harvey, and Thomas Campion. These poets wanted to refine English verse, not revolutionize it.

That is, they wanted to produce verse in which the two systems—native accented prosody and what they called "reformed" quantitative prosody—could be made to correspond. What they termed "artificial verse," that is, English verse written according to the principles of Latin verse taught in schools, was to be nearly indistinguishable from English verse constructed according to accents. Because these early modern writers were not interested in exploiting the clash between these systems, it is sometimes difficult to determine which versification principles apply to particular poems.[1]

A.2.1. What constitutes a long syllable in English is variable, and writers of quantitative verse define such syllables differently. Thus to determine the verse form used by a writer, it is often necessary to proceed not *from* prosodic considerations to the verse form but rather *toward* the prosodic considerations that are at the base of a given (or hypothesized) verse form. One indication that a verse is written according to quantity is simply that it will not scan according to patterns of accent.

A.3. Two Forms of Elegiac Couplet
A.3.1. Sidney's elegiacs are based directly on the classical form:

> Unto a caitif wretch, whom long affliction holdeth,
> > and now fully believ's help to be quite perished,
> Grant yet, grant yet a look, to the last moment of his anguish,
> > O you (alas so I finde) caus of his onely ruine.
>
> > > > > > (*Arcadia,* bk. 3)

The first couplet is a dactylic hexameter followed by the pentameter of a classical elegiac couplet. Both lines can be scanned by quantity

---

1. One of the explicit principles for the determination of a quantitatively long syllable was the accent itself. "Above all the accent of our words is diligently to be observ'd, for chiefly by the accent in any language the true value of the syllables is to be measured" (Campion). By "true value," Campion means the quantity of the syllable, long or short. The coincidence of accent and quantity in such cases meant that clashes of the two systems were relatively infrequent. See Thomas Campion, *Observations in the Art of English Poesie (1602)* in Smith, 2:351.

and perhaps by accent as well; all syllables that receive a stress accent are also counted long in the quantitative scansion (although some unstressed syllables are counted long). This might be indicated as follows:

$$- \quad \smile \ \smile |{\underline{}} \ -| - \qquad - \ | - \ -| - \ \smile\smile \ |- \ >$$
Unto a caitif wretch, whom long affliction holdeth,
$$- \qquad -| \ -\smile \ \smile |- \ \| - \ \smile \ \smile| \ - \ -|-$$
and now fully believ's help to be quite perished,

The pentameter of the second couplet can only be scanned properly according to quantity:

$$- \ \smile \ \smile |{\underline{}} \ \smile \smile |- \ \| \qquad - \quad \smile \ \smile| \ -\smile \ \smile| -$$
O you (alas so I finde)   cause of his only ruine

The accent of "ruine" on the first syllable clashes with the required quantitative scansion, whereby this is an iamb (the first syllable is short, the second long). The lines are thus written in quantitative meter.

A.3.2. Campion's version of elegiac couplet is more complex. Campion wished to use lines that he considered natural to English and, like many writers, described natural English rhythm as iambic (it is not entirely clear whether he meant that this iambic rhythm is quantitative or accentual). Campion's elegiac couplet is composed not of dactylic verse but of two iambic verse types, which he defines as a "licentiate iambick" followed by a line constructed of two "dimeters."

A.3.2.1. Campion's "licentiate iambick" is close to what is loosely known as iambic pentameter; his description of this verse is reminiscent of descriptions of the Latin iambic senarius (see chap. 2, F).[2] According to Campion, there are three forms of this iambic line, beginning with a basic form:

---

2. Campion's Latin examples are unfortunately mis-scanned; see Smith, 2:334.

⌣ — | ⌣ — | ⌣ — | ⌣ — | ⌣ —

In the second form, which Campion calls the "licentiate" form, substitutions are permitted in feet 1, 2, and 4; for the iamb, one can substitute a spondee, tribrach, or dactyl but, as in the Latin senarius, not a trochee (that is, one can substitute a short for a long or resolve any long into two shorts). Anapests, I believe, are permitted in feet 2 and 4 but not 1. Foot 3 and foot 5 must be pure iambs. There is, according to Campion, a break after syllable 4, what Campion calls a "naturall breathing-place." These possible substitutions might be represented as follows:

⌣ — | ⌣ — | ⌣ — | ⌣ — | ⌣ —
— —   — —   — —
          ⌣ ⌣ —   ⌣ ⌣ —
— ⌣ ⌣ — ⌣ ⌣   — ⌣ ⌣
⌣ ⌣ ⌣ ⌣ ⌣ ⌣   ⌣ ⌣ ⌣

In a most tantalizing note, Campion identifies a third form by suggesting that more license is permitted in verse comedy. Such a form would permit free substitution in any of the feet, including 3 and 5, and Campion's implied forms of "iambick" would be roughly analogous to the forms of iambic senarius in Latin. Unfortunately, Campion gives no examples. Was he thinking of the verse of his contemporary English dramatists?

A.3.2.2. *Dimeter.* Campion defines a dimeter as a line that consists of two feet plus an extra syllable. The first foot is generally a trochee (a spondee or iamb may be substituted); the second a trochee or tribrach; the last foot "common." Campion gives the following example:

> Raving warre, begot
> In the thirstye sands
> Of the *Lybian* Iles,
> Wasts our emptye fields

Line 1 in Campion's analysis likely includes a spondee for foot 1 and is scanned — — | — ⌣ | >. The opening prepositions in lines 2 and 3 are perhaps "long by position" (a vowel is followed by a consonant combination).

A.3.2.3. Campion's version of elegiac couplet is thus composed of two problematic line types: a "licentiate iambick" (the second of the three forms of iambic described above in sec. A.3.2.1) followed by a line composed of two dimeters:

> Constant to none, but ever false to me
>> Traitor still to love through thy faint desires
> Not hope to pittie now nor vaine redresse
>> Turns my griefs to teares and renu'd laments.
>>>> (Campion, "An Elegy")

I believe Campion intends this to be scanned as follows:

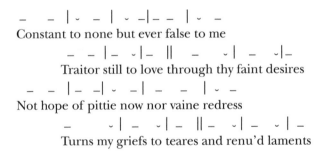

I frankly could not and would not scan it precisely that way without Campion's description. As in Sidney, there is almost no conflict of accent and quantity.

A.4. English Sapphics
For the most part, English writers adopted a generalized form of Ae-olic verse in what became known as the Horatian ode—short, four-line, rhymed stanzas written on themes common to the verse of Horace (discussed in chap. 5, B.2.1). Exceptional is the Sapphic. The form is easily imitated visually as a four-line stanza of three repeated lines followed by a shorter concluding line, generally of the form _ ˇ ˇ (quantitative version) or ´ x x (accentual version). The various ways of adapting the form to English are shown below.

A.4.1. William Webbe (quantitative form):

— ⏑ —   — — ⏑ ⏑ — ⏑ — —

O ye Nymphes most fine, who resort to this brooke,
For to bathe there your pretty breasts at all times,
Leave the watrish bowres, hyther and to me come
        at my request nowe.
        (Webbe, trans., Edmund Spenser,
        The Shepheardes Calender, from Smith, 1:287)

A.4.2. Algernon Charles Swinburne, "Sapphics" (accentual form):

´ x ´ ´ ´ x x ´ x ´ x

All the night sleep came not upon my eyelids,
Shed not dew, nor shoo nor unclosed a feather,
Yet with lips shut close and with eyes of iron
        Stood and beheld me

A.4.3. William Hyde Appleton, trans., "Hymn to Aphrodite" (1893):

Throned in splendor, immortal Aphrodite!
Child of Zeus, Enchantress, I implore thee
Slay me not in this distress and anguish
        Lady of beauty.

This last case, I believe in decasyllables, could be called an allusion to the Sapphic stanza in its visual form and in the rhythm of its last line. Many similar examples were probably written as school exercises or in the spirit of school exercises ("Turn the following prose passage into Sapphics . . .").

B. Syllabic and Isosyllabic Verse Forms
B.1. Heroic Couplet
The following is one of the few cases where my own analysis is not compatible with standard sources on metrics. Since the eighteenth century, histories of English verse have associated the rhymed verse found in Chaucer's *Canterbury Tales* with the heroic couplet of Dryden and Pope. Such couplets are now generally described as pairs

of rhyming lines in iambic pentameter, and the main point of contention in literary histories is whether this tradition is continuous, that is, whether the decasyllabic couplets in the *Canterbury Tales* are variants of the form used by Dryden and Pope. While the association of Chaucer's verse with that of Dryden and Pope is reasonable (both Dryden and Pope read and translated Chaucer), the labeling of all this verse as rhymed iambic pentameter is misleading. To Dryden himself, who translated Chaucer into rhyming couplets in 1700, Chaucer's verses were syllabic: his "Numbers" were occasionally deficient in that they lacked the requisite number of ten syllables a line. This is exactly how Chaucer characterizes his own verse, apologizing in his *Hous of Fame* for lines that "fail in a syllable." And whereas some scholars give Chaucer credit for inventing what is now known as the heroic couplet, to Dryden, neither Chaucer nor English poets in general invented anything: "The Genius of our Countrymen being rather to improve an Invention, than to invent themselves" (from Preface, *Fables Ancient and Modern*, 1700).

B.1.1. The notion of a specifically English tradition here—that is, the idea that Chaucer wrote and perhaps invented a verse form later perfected by Pope, a verse that can be described as both foot-based and accentual—may well misrepresent the principles and bases of both types of verse. This notion begins with the assumption of a basic iambic, accentual form. A better and equally workable definition of this form of couplet is that the couplets of Chaucer and Pope are fundamentally decasyllabic lines written according to principles articulated in French poetics and exemplified in French verse. Chaucer's and Pope's couplets are similar not because they have a direct relation but because both are based on the French verse of their near contemporaries. Thus the English decasyllable as found in Chaucer and Pope can be described in the same notation used for French decasyllables of any period:

$$x \; x \; x \; X \; \| \; x \; x \; x \; x \; x \; X \; (x)$$

Chaucer, far from the inventor of heroic couplet, simply copies the French decasyllable, with the *rhymes plates* one finds in octosyllabic narrative. The iambic accentual rhythm one finds in a Chaucerian decasyllable can be considered a secondary (ornamental?) function that is added to the basic structure of the line. In Pope, there is almost without exception an accent on syllable 4 and a break (caesura or *coupe*) following either accented syllable 4 or unaccented syllable 5. Syntax inevitably follows line structure, that is, a full stop follows each couplet. Pope's heroic couplet, then, is an Anglicization in decasyllabic form of the classical French Alexandrine.

B.1.1.1. Chaucer:

> The lyf so short, the craft so long to lerne,
> Th'assay so hard, so sharp the conquering,
> The dredful joye, that alwey slit so yerne,
> Al this mene I by love, that my feling
> Astonyeth with this wonderful worching
> So sore y-wis, that whan I on him thinke,
> Nat wot I wel wher that I wake or winke.
>
> (*Parlement of Fowles*)

We could of course describe these lines as iambic pentameter, but to do so implies that Chaucer invented this meter, one for which Chaucer had no precedent. And Chaucer has an obvious precedent here: the stanzaic form, *rime royale*, is borrowed directly from the French; it is likely that the line structure, with the implied caesura following syllable 4, was borrowed as well. There is nothing here that cannot be analyzed in terms of the general rules for French decasyllable discussed above in chapter 3.

The couplets in the *Canterbury Tales* are just a further refinement, and there is less evidence of a caesura:

> Whan that Aprille with his shoures sote
> The droghte of Marche hath perced to the rote,
> And bathed every veyne in swich licour,
> Of which vertu engendred is the flour.
>
> (General Prologue)

It might also be possible to see *Troilus and Criseyde* as a variant of Italian hendecasyllable, which we know Chaucer had before him as he wrote this poem.

To define Chaucer's couplets as versions of a uniquely English form of iambic pentameter based on stress is to claim that Chaucer invented this unexampled verse form. More important, it requires us to believe that while doing this, Chaucer managed to ignore the nearly identical verse forms (French decasyllabic verse, Italian hendecasyllables) that were immediately before his eyes as he wrote.

B.1.1.2. Pope:

> 'Tis hard to say, if greater Want of Skill
> Appear in Writing, or in Judging ill,
> But, of the two, less dang'rous is th' Offence
> To tire our Patience, than mis-lead our Sense.
>
> (*Essay on Criticism*)

The easiest and simplest way to describe the form of Pope's couplets is according to the rules of French decasyllabic verse (chap. 3): ten syllables, with a required accent on syllables 4 and 10 and caesura following syllable 4 or unaccented (post-tonic) syllable 5: x x x X ‖ x x x x x X, or x x x X x ‖ x x x x X.[3] This syllabic description is not incompatible with standard descriptions of the dreaded iambic pentameter. But it seems to me much easier to begin with a system that allows variation (decasyllable with two required stresses), rather than propose a system (iambic pentameter) in which almost every line must be analyzed as an exception.

B.1.2. The rules for writing French verse were known and articulated by contemporaries of both Chaucer and Pope, and both poets read and studied French poems written according to these principles. Chaucer translated and wrote versions of poems by Deschamps and Machaut; Pope's *Essay on Criticism* (1711) is a version of Boileau's *Art of Poetry* (1673). One can certainly argue that the verse forms of Chaucer and Pope are specifically English and describe them further as a system of alternating WS, classical iambic pentameter, or a

---

3. This is similar to but not strictly a lyric caesura, which in French medieval verse follows unaccented syllable 4.

strange verse of four primary stresses. But why would one do this? The verse can be described just as easily by applying the principles of the very texts they translate: French texts in syllabic form. To ignore this entails arguing that the formal relation to the French sources is somehow (and very mysteriously) coincidental.

B.2. Purely Isosyllabic Verse

In This Age of Hard Trying, Nonchalance is Good and

"really it is not the
business of the gods to bake clay pots." They did not
do it in this instance. A few
revolved upon the axes of their worth
as if excessive popularity might be a pot;

they did not venture the
profession of humility. The polished wedge
that might have split the firmament
was dumb. At last it threw itself away
and falling down, conferred on some poor fool, a privilege. . . .

(Marianne Moore)

To understand isosyllabic verse structure, one needs only to compare multiple stanzas: the metrical rules here define a stanza consisting of lines of six, twelve, eight, ten, and fourteen syllables. These lines are purely isosyllabic; that is, they are constructed solely according to the number of syllables, without regard to syllable quantity, accent, or syntax. Such lines are occasionally said to be based on French principles. But as noted in chapter 3, the only French verse that could be described as purely isosyllabic is experimental verse, such as that written by Verlaine in the late nineteenth century. All classical and romantic French verse has supplemental rules regarding accent, caesura, and even syntax, and line length is defined by the position of a terminal tonic accent, not by syllable count alone (that is, a ten-syllable line is defined as one with a terminal tonic accent on syllable 10, but one that may have more than ten syllables). The experimental isosyllabic verse of Moore and Robert Bridges (often mentioned in this context) has little to do with this.

C. Accentual Verse: Sprung Rhythm

The most notable example of modern accentual verse is what is often called "sprung rhythm" as found in Gerard Manley Hopkins. The term is invented by Hopkins himself in his 1918 Preface, where he describes his poems as written in various forms: some are written in "common English rhythm, called Running Rhythm," others in "Sprung Rhythm," and still others in mixtures of the two.

C.1. Hopkins's Description

Although Hopkins shows some familiarity with theories of early Germanic verse, in his preface he describes his own version in classical terms. Lines consist of feet, and these feet consist of two elements, essentially what in classical meter are called the *arsis* and *thesis,* which Hopkins translates as "Stress" and "Slack." "Every foot has one principal stress or accent, and this or the syllable it falls on may be called the Stress of the foot and the other part . . . the Slack." There are thus two theoretical types of feet, "rising" and "falling," that is, those with the stress on the second element, or those with stress on the first. In a striking note, Hopkins then shifts his ground from classical metrics to classical musical notation: "for purposes of scanning it is a great convenience to follow the example of music and take the stress always first, as the accent or the chief accent always comes first in a musical bar." This effectively eliminates the notion of iambic or anapestic rhythm.

C.1.1. Hopkins describes sprung rhythm as follows:

> Sprung rhythm, as used in this book, is measured by feet of from one to four syllables, regularly, and for particular effects any number of weak or slack syllables may be used. It [the foot] has one stress, which falls on the only syllable, if there is only one, or, if there are more, then scanning as above, on the first, and so gives rise to four sorts of feet, a monosyllable and the so-called accentual Trochee, Dactyl, and the First Paeon. And there will be four corresponding natural rhythms. (Preface)

These rhythms might be represented as X, X x, X x x, X x x x or ´, ´ x, ´ x x, ´ x x x, where x indicates a syllable. In the above formulation, "rhythm" logically applies to individual feet, although it is not clear how such a thing as monosyllabic rhythm is possible. The rhythm of any particular line would necessarily consist of a combination of these four rhythms.

A poet can also bring in "licenses," "as in the common ten-syllable or five-foot verse." For sprung rhythm, Hopkins defines two licenses: rests as in music (although Hopkins claims he doesn't use these), and "hangers or outrides," that is, one, two, or three unstressed syllables (Hopkins's "slack" syllables) added to a foot.

C.1.2. Hopkins indicates his rhythms typographically with diacritical marks and accents "where the reader might be in doubt which syllable should have the stress; slurs . . . little loops at the end of a line to shew that the rhyme goes on to the first letter of the next line." Modern editions of Hopkins rarely include these marks.

C.2. Examples

In the context of the forms described here, we can see Hopkins as a proponent of accentual verse, through what I have called "allusions" to early Germanic alliterative verse. When describing accentual verse in his preface, however, Hopkins makes no mention of alliteration and what to modern readers is the most obvious feature of both his and early Germanic lines.

> Look at the stars! look, look up at the skies!
> O look at all the fire-folk sitting in the air!
> the bright boroughs, the circle-citadels there?
> Down in dim woods the diamond delves! the elves eyes!
> (Hopkins, "The Starlight Night")

A line, as described by Hopkins, is composed of a predetermined number of feet, which is the same as the number of accents (although it is not quite in accord with Hopkins's own language to speak of a line as containing a particular number of accents). But how one would determine these accents is not clear: even with Hopkins's typographical aids, this is often anyone's guess. Some lines can be reasonably analyzed as containing five stresses (or is it four?):

The bright boroughs, the circle-citadels there?[4]

In this case, the metrical stress falls on alliterating or potentially al-literating elements, just as it would in earlier Germanic verse. But other lines have alliterating elements presumably on an unstressed syllable: is the scansion of the last line as follows?

Down in the dim woods the diamond delves! the elves eyes!

Are we to ignore the implied stress on, say, "woods"? or the visual al-literation of the last two words? And in line 1, are we to pronounce the phrase "Look up" as part of a "falling foot" (thus leaving the syn-tactic emphasis on the word "up" unstressed?), leaving us with three stresses on the repeated word "look" and two more on "stars" and "skies"?

C.3. Precedents

Hopkins claimed his verse had classical and medieval precedent in Greek and Latin lyric verse and in "the old English verse seen in *Pierce Ploughman*" (a verse that Hopkins asserts ceased to be used since the Elizabethan Age). The classical precedent claimed by Hop-kins is likely in the mixture of trochaic and dactylic feet, which, fol-lowing contemporary descriptions of classical verse, Hopkins calls *logaoedic* verse, a form that combines "spoken" and "lyric" metrical elements. The term is no longer used in most classical manuals, and without it, the classical underpinnings of Hopkins's verse may well disappear. It would be very difficult to describe his verse according to the language used in these manuals, and to do so would only ob-scure what Hopkins's himself felt was the classical basis of his verse— the indifferent mixture of feet.

---

4. To describe this line in Hopkins's own terms likely requires invoking the term *anacrusis* to describe the unstressed opening syllable "The"; the first foot would then be the monosyllabic "Bright," the second foot the dactylic "boroughs the," etc.

The early Germanic precedent for Hopkins is equally problematic, since the most prominent element, the alliteration, while clearly imitated by Hopkins, plays no part in his descriptions. The coincidence of stress and alliteration found in early Germanic verse and in verse of the so-called alliterative revival seems of secondary importance. Did Hopkins regard this feature of his verse, the most prominent feature for most modern readers, purely a matter of ornamentation? Or are we to see this verse, like other revived types, rooted in a creative misrepresentation of past forms?

C.4. Ezra Pound, "The Seafarer"

I close with an easier and far more amusing case. Pound's translation of *The Seafarer* is a product of his early enthusiasm for languages. Although it is easy to share in this enthusiasm, it was also unfashionable among Anglo-Saxonists to admit such enthusiasm, as I discovered on more than one professional occasion:

> May I for my own self song's truth reckon,
> Journey's jargon, how I in harsh days
> Hardship endured oft.
> Bitter breast-cares have I abided,
> Known on my keel many a care's hold . . .

This is a good example of allusion to form rather than imposition of form. Pound was surely exposed to Sievers's half-line types in his Old English studies, but I doubt he could have passed a test on them, nor much cared about them.[5] What he presents in this translation is (1) the alliteration he saw: "self song's"; "journey's jargon"; "Known on my keel, many a care's hold"; and (2) what was convenient to represent: thus the perfectly literal "Bitter breast-cares || have I abided." As a whole, Pound's *Seafarer* seems to represent not the Old English poem but rather the enthusiastic student's effort to translate the Old English poem, perhaps in a parody of Hopkins's own neo-gothic verse. This might explain the very elements so disparaged by serious Anglo-Saxon scholars, among whom Pound never pretended to be

---

5. For example, the forbidden X x x X half-line type frequent here.

numbered: the wildly divergent formal elements; alliterating, strongly rhythmic lines combined with pedestrian prose; serious translations combined with the type of puns and jokes common among those learning a new language; parodic archaisms ("daring ado," "Delight 'mid the doughty"). What is shown is not the real formal or even linguistic basis of the poem but the brilliant student's inability or unwillingness to grasp it.

D. Songs of John Donne

Lyrics to songs are analogous to what are known as "shape poems," in that both are constructed on the basis of extraliterary forms. In a shape poem, the principle of organization is the physical shape of the printed or written words. When the text of such a poem is reproduced apart from that shape, there is little hope of recovering its exact organizing principle. A classical example in English is George Herbert's "The Altar" (1633):

> A broken ALTAR, Lord, thy servant rears
> Made of a heart, and cemented with tears
> Whose parts are as thy hand did frame;
> No workmans tool hath touch'd the same.
> A   HEART   alone
> Is   such   a   stone,
> As   nothing   but
> Thy pow'r doth cut,
> Wherefore each part
> Of my hard heart
> Meets in this frame,
> To praise thy name
> That if I chance to hold my peace,
> These songes to praise thee may not cease.
> O let thy blessed SACRIFICE be mine
> And sanctifie this ALTAR to be thine.

If this poem were printed apart from its shape, its underlying *raison d'être* might well be lost. Lyrics to songs are similar. If the song underlying a lyric is unknown, its versification will be unknown (and readers must be content with that).

The best we can do in such cases is to know that a musical basis (or implied musical basis) exists. And there are many clues that suggest that some such musical system is operable. Among these are:

a) *title* (e.g., "Song")

b) *line length;* before the late nineteenth-century poems written in odd-numbered lines are often intended to be sung or have a musical form at their base.

c) *seemingly random line combinations;* most stanzas that are not formed in obvious patterns have a musical base or, like the English romantic ode, allude to one. John Donne's familiar "Song" shows all these characteristics:[6]

> Goe, and catche a falling starre,
>> Get with child a mandrake roote,
> Tell me, where all past yeares are,
>> Or who cleft the Divels foot,
> Teach me to heare Mermaides singing,
>> Or to keep off envies stinging,
>>> And finde
>>> What winde
> Serves to advance an honest minde.

The printer distinguishes three types of line here, but we have no way of knowing whether what the printer thought was true; in subsequent stanzas, these are set differently, in a pattern that suggests line lengths as follows: 7, 7, 7, 7, 8, 8, 2, 2, 7.

The stanzas in a second Donne "Song" ("Sweetest love, I do not go") are similar:

> Sweetest love, I do not go
>> For wearinesse of thee,
> Nor in hope the world can show
>> A fitter Love for me,
>> But since that I

---

6. I quote the 1633 edition, not because it is authoritative, which it is not, but because the spelling is sometimes more apt to indicate actual line structure than that of modern editions.

Must die at last, 'tis best
To use myself in jest
    Thus by fain'd deaths to dye . . .

Here, we have lines of four, six, and seven syllables, with relatively simple syntax. Although we do not know the music behind this stanza, we know that it is not purely experimental, nor is it built on iambic, trochaic, or more abstruse "logaoedic" forms; it is simply the lyrical embodiment of a preexistent song.

More elaborate and problematic versions include Donne's "The Message":

Send home my long strayd eyes to mee,
Which (Oh) too long have dwelt on thee,
Yet since there they have learn'd such ill,
    Such forc'd fashions,
    And false passions
      That they be
      Made by thee
Fit for no good fight, keep them still.

The three-syllable lines seem clearly related to those in the previous songs. But the possible musical basis is belied by the somewhat more difficult syntax: could such a poem be understood if sung? And from a stanza such as this, it is a short step to the following familiar stanza from Donne's "Canonization":

For Godsake hold your tongue, and let me love,
    Or chide my palsie, or my gout,
My five gray haires, or ruin'd fortune flout
  With wealth your state, your minde with Arts improve
    Take you a course, get you a place,
    Observe his honour, or his grace,
Or the Kings reall, or his stamped face
    Contemplate, what you will, approve,
    So you will let me love.

Here, the difficulty of the syntax, as well as the subject matter in later stanzas, speaks against a literal musical background; and it is interesting, looking through Donne poems comparable to this one in difficulty, that most show lines of even-numbered syllables. Again, the rule of the odd-syllable line indicating a musical background for French and English poems may apply. Somewhere in this progression of poems, Donne's use of musical background becomes purely metaphorical, and he exploits the apparent freedom provided by musically based stanzaic forms. Such poems then are similar to the sonnet and the nearly contemporary English ode discussed in chapter 5, B.

| For the modern reader, verses with a musical basis are simple to detect: they are in short repeating stanzas; if there are three or more stanzas, it is a simple matter to determine scribal or printing errors or even curiosities of pronunciation. Each line in each stanza will have the same number of syllables, and each stanza will incorporate the same rhyme scheme. Nothing is to be gained by a more elaborate formal analysis involving inverted feet, substitutions, etc. And we would be better off, perhaps, writing a pseudo-Elizabethan song to accompany them than to burden them with the classical and too-often standard language of versification.

Texts: English texts from the facsimile images of early editions in Early English Books Online, eebo.chadwyck.com, and from Literature Online, lionchadwyck .com; texts of Gerard Manley Hopkins are from *Poems* (1918), www.bartleby .com/122/100.

References: John Dryden, preface to *Fables, Ancient and Modern* (London, 1700); G. Gregory Smith, ed. *Elizabethan Critical Essays,* 2 vols. (Oxford: Clarendon Press, 1904).

Conclusion

A Note to Teachers of English

So what to do now? Students may be mildly curious about French or Old English verse, but their main literary energies are more likely to be spent elsewhere. What about English verse?

A. Basic Terminology

First and foremost, we should stop discussing and teaching English versification in the traditional language of feet and foot types found in handbooks. Students do not understand how to distinguish trochaic from iambic lines even in cases where the distinction is meaningful; they don't know what a foot means or why people think it is important; they don't know Greek terminology; and when they write verse, they don't think in these terms. In consequence, Iambic Pentameter really, really needs to go. When I heard the best student in one of my classes use this term as a synonym for verse itself ("the iambic pentameter in this line consists of five syllables"), whatever tolerance I may have once had for it vanished.

Second, we should concede that English verse is not uniform; different poems and verse types are based on different and sometimes conflicting principles. Even in the limited number of cases discussed here, different language and different notation has to be employed to describe different verse types. We cannot expect language that works to describe one system (say, Greek epic) to describe another, nor should we believe those who claim it does.

Finally, we need to accept the fact that much is simply unknown. We can articulate the rules for a classical Latin dactylic hexameter or a French Alexandrine; but this does not mean that we should expect to do the same for a line in Shakespeare. And this of course has nothing to do with the relative virtues of Latin, French, and English verse, any more than our confusion about the afterlife has anything to do with how grand it might well be.

B. Traditional Language of Verse

Before teaching or learning anything, it is well to consider why we are doing that. What are the reasons to teach or to learn such things as trochees, iambs, dactyls, and anapests? This terminology is extremely useful for teaching classical metrics; it has been used since the earliest treatises on Greek and Latin verse were written, and it has a continuous history of use through the twentieth century. As a consequence of their classical education, many English poets were exposed to this language and may have internalized it the same way they internalized the principles of classical verse from the beatings they received when they did not. There are thus times when knowledge of this language is useful: if one is interested in the formal origins of Longfellow's *Hiawatha*, it is a good idea to know what trochaic tetrameter is. Furthermore, for better or worse, standard handbooks on verse in English use this language. To understand, say, a mid-century handbook on poetics, a cursory knowledge of classical terminology is essential. But the cases in the history of English poetry where knowledge of this traditional language is necessary or even helpful are very few. Unless a poem at hand is written specifically in imitation of classical metrical forms, or unless one's interest is in the history of descriptions of versification rather than in versification itself, there is little reason to invoke this language or to ask anyone to learn it.

C. Line and Syllable

Poems are constructed in visual patterns that distinguish them from prose, and any paragraph typeset in lines (or in any other shape) is different from the same paragraph set continuously. But metrically, a poem is no less a poem if it reads like prose when typed as prose. The most familiar poem pattern involves repeating lines and is called "verse"—the word itself is part of a plowing metaphor: when you reach the end of a furrow, you have to reverse the plow to start the adjacent one, and what you end up with is a field of plowed rows. The lines of most Western poems are actually or potentially repeatable, and poets mark that repeatability in different ways: by terminal rhyme, line or syllable length, the number of accents, or even the number of *r*'s if they want. Or, they can simply hit the return button.

The easiest and least controversial way to analyze the form of poems written in verse and to discover the basis of this repeatability is simply to count the syllables in each line. It will not take long to discover that most English poems use lines of six, eight, or ten syllables. The same types of variation are used in English that we have seen in other languages. Feminine endings, unaccented endings, and post-tonic endings in an English line generally result in an extra syllable. Sometimes two unaccented syllables count as one. If a poem is written according to different principles (say, a late Middle English alliterative poem), that will quickly reveal itself.

C.1. Examples

English poets keep track of the number of syllables in different ways. Some poems are based heavily on accent, as in the English ballads of the eighteenth century and in this version by Coleridge:

> In Xanadu did Kubla Khan
> A stately Pleasure Dome decree,
> Through caverns measureless to Man
> Down to the soundless Sea.
> > ("Kubla Khan")

I count eight, eight, eight, and six syllables in these lines. The close of each line is marked by a terminal accent and a rhyme. The first three lines are perhaps organized by accent: four of them. The last has three. If one wants now to speak of "iambic" rhythm in the first three lines, that will probably not do any particular harm, but it probably will do little good.

In poems where the metrical basis is uncertain, it is often useful to begin with syllable count. The following stanza is by Wallace Stevens:

> Call the roller of big cigars
> The muscular one, and bid him whip
> In kitchen cups concupiscent curds.
> Let the wenches dawdle in such dress
> As they are used to wear . . .
> > ("The Emperor of Ice Cream")

Lines of eight, eight, eight, and nine syllables. Each line ends with a terminal stress that rhymes. Each line has four accents. In the second and last stanza of the poem the number of syllables varies between eight and ten. There remain four accents.

Other poems are constructed around a variable caesura following a regularly accented syllable:

> Not with more Glories, in th' Ethereal Plain,
> The Sun first rises o'er the purpled Main,
> Than issuing forth, the Rival of his Beams
> Launch'd on the Bosom of the Silver Thames.
> > (Pope, "The Rape of the Lock")

The above lines regularly show accent on syllable 4 and a caesura after syllable 4 or unaccented syllable 5.

Some poets may keep track simply by counting:

> Of man's first disobedience and the Fruit
> of that Forbidden Tree, whose mortal taste
> Brought Death into the world and all our woe . . .
> > (Milton, *Paradise Lost*, bk. 1)

Ten syllables, with an accent on syllable 10; no caesura, no accentual pattern, no rhyme. If this were written as prose, it would not be possible to reconstruct the meter. If you follow a handbook, this will be called blank verse.

Other poets do not keep track at all:

> I saw the best minds of my generation destroyed by
>   madness, starving hysterical naked,
> dragging themselves through the negro streets at dawn
>   looking for an angry fix,
> angelheaded hipsters burning for the ancient heavenly
>   connection to the starry dynamo in the machinery
>   of night
>
> (Allen Ginsberg, *Howl*)

I have no idea how many syllables each line has because I lose count. A new line is one that is written or typeset as a new line.

There is clearly a continuum here. Some poets use a very regular and pronounced line structure, defined by syllable count and reinforced by accent. Others use a loose system of syllable count. Others simply start a new line, perhaps (radically!) one that begins with a lowercase letter.

C.1.1. Shakespeare

When we come to Shakespeare, and we must, using this plain language to describe what is before us should not prove difficult:

> When my love swears that she is made of truth,
> I do believe her though I know she lies,
> That she might think me some untutor'd youth,
> Unlearned in the world's false subtleties.
>
> (Sonnet 138)

Ten-syllable lines (possibly aided by alternative pronunciation of "unlearnèd" and "untutor'd"), terminal accent supported by rhyme. No caesura, no apparent required accent.

Shakespeare's plays have a different metrical basis. The main evidence that Shakespeare writes in regular accented (iambic) decasyllables is from his parodies of them, as in this rhymed version from the play-within-a-play in *Hamlet*:

Full thirtie times hath Phoebus Cart gon round,
Neptunes salt Wash, and Tullus Orbed ground:
And thirtie dozen Moones with borrowed sheene,
About the World have times twelve thirties beene . . .

(act 3, sc. 2)

One could also cite this unrhymed passage from *Love's Labour's Lost*:

Thus poure the stars down plagues for periury.
Can any face of brasse hold longer out?
Heere stand I, Ladie dart thy skill at me,
Bruise me with scorne, confound me with a flout.

(act 5, sc. 2)

In some cases, the notion of iambic decasyllables might prove useful in analyzing particular passages from his plays. In other cases, it will not:

Thou Nature art my Godesse, to thy Law
My services are bound, wherefore should I
Stand in the plague of custome, and permit
The curiosity of Nations, to deprive me?
For that I am some twelve, or fourteene Moonshines
Lag of a Brother? Why Bastard? Wherefore base?

(*King Lear*, act 1, sc. 2)

Our models above are of little help. Is the basic line here ten syllables? or is it eleven? or thirteen? There is an answer to this question: *we don't know.* The above text is from the the 1623 First Folio, the version found in most printed editions today. But the two earlier quartos do not agree. They print this same speech as prose. This is only one of many cases in Shakespeare's plays where equally reliable textual authorities disagree on what constitutes a verse line, or whether there is any verse line at all.

D. Performance

Finally, a word about performance. For English, the simplest, plainest description of any given verse is never a bad idea: line x has ten syllables with an accent on the last one. That description, of course, will not tell you how to read a line aloud, any more than your third-year French course will tell you how to read particular lines of Corneille. But it will put the fewest constraints on reading or performance. The discussion of whether to stress "thy" in line 1 of Edmund's soliloquy from *King Lear* quoted above is a matter for actors and the literary critics on whose opinions all actors rely; it is not a matter of concern for those who study metrics and versification. Versification is not as difficult or mysterious as these other fields. A student of versification is concerned only, say, with prosodic value (e.g., *Nature* is a two syllable word with stress on syllable 1); how that prosodic value is realized in performance is a matter for those who perform it. Overly rich and complex metrical language involving such things as multiple levels of emphasis or stress (primary, secondary, tertiary, relative . . .) should thus be looked at skeptically; it is often no more than a guide to performance, something like the suggested fingerings in a Schirmer piano score.

| I have no doubt that many students will still not "get" meter when it is presented this way. But at least this will be because verse itself is of no interest to them, or because the subject is too simple. They will certainly develop no more respect for literature or interest in it if our language suggests that its simplest formal elements constitute some kind of mystery religion to which they can never hope to become initiates.

Appendix

Examples and Scansion of Common Verse Types

Chapter 2: Quantitative Verse

D.1. Dactylic Hexameter

   _ ˘ ˘ | _ ˘ ˘| _ ˘ ˘ | _ _ | _ ˘ ˘ | _ >
Tītyre, tū patulae recubāns sub tegmine fāgi
   _ _ | _ ˘ ˘| _ _| _ ˘ ˘ | _ ˘ ˘ | _ >
silvestrem tenuī mūsam meditāris avēna:
   _ ˘ ˘ | _ _| _ _ | _ ˘ ˘| _ ˘ ˘ | _ >
nōs patriae fīnīs et dulcia linquimus arva.
   _ ˘ ˘ | _ ˘ ˘ | _ _ | _ ˘ ˘ | _ ˘ ˘ | _ >
nōs patriam fugimus: tū, Tītyre, lentus in umbrā
   _ _ | _ ˘ ˘ | _ ˘ ˘ | _ ˘ ˘ | _ ˘ ˘ | _ >
formōsam resonāre docēs Amaryllida silvās.
   _ ˘ ˘ | _ ˘ ˘ | _ _| _ _ | _ ˘˘ | _ >
T: Ō Meliboee, deus nōbis haec ōtia fēcit.
   _ ˘ ˘| _ ˘ ˘ | _ _ | _ ˘ ˘ | _ ˘ ˘| _ >
namque erit ille mihī semper deus, illius āram
   _ ˘ ˘ | _ _| _ ˘ ˘ ˘| _ _ ˘ | _ ˘ ˘| _ >
saepe tener nostrīs ab ovīlibus imbuet agnus.
   _ ˘ ˘| _ _| _ ˘ ˘ ˘| _ _ | _ ˘ ˘| _ >
ille meās errāre bovēs, ut cernis, et ipsum
   _ ˘ ˘ | _ _ | _ ˘ ˘| _ _| _ ˘ ˘ | _ >
lūdere quae vellem calamō permīsit agrestī.

                      (Vergil, *Eclogues* 1)

———

[Tityrus, lying under the cover of a spreading beech, you
exercise the silvestran muse with a tender reed; we have
left the sweet borders and fields of our fatherland: you,
Tityrus, relaxed in the shade, teach the woods to resound
with the name of Amaryllis.
O Meliboeus, god gave us this peace. For he will always
be a god to me; often a tender lamb from our flocks stains
his altar. He allows my cattle to roam as you see, and me
to play where I wish with the country reed.]

All lines above show caesura in foot 3, and the majority show *bucolic
diaeresis* (a coincidence of word break and foot break between foot 4
and foot 5).

D.2. Elegiac Couplet

$$- \; \smile \; \smile \,|\, - \; \smile \; \smile \,|\, - \; \smile\smile \,|\, - \; \smile \; \smile \,|\, \; - \; \smile \; \smile \,|\, - >$$
Arma gravī numerō violentaque bella parābam

$$- \; \smile\smile \,|\, - \; \smile\smile \,|\, - \,\|\, - \; \smile\smile \,|\, \smile \; \smile \,|\, >$$
ēdere, māteriā   conveniente modīs.

$$- \; \smile \smile \,|\, - \; \smile \; \smile \,|\, - \; - \,|\, - \; \; - \,|\, \smile \; \smile \,|\, - >$$
pār erat inferior versus; rīsisse Cupīdō

$$- \; \smile \smile \,|\, - \; \; - \,|\, \; - \,\|\, - \; \smile \; \smile \,|\, - \; \smile \,|\, >$$
dīcitur atque ūnum   surripuisse pedem.

$$- \; \; \smile\smile \,|\, - \; \smile \; \smile \,|\, - \; \smile\smile \,|\, - \; \; - \,|\, - \; \smile \; \smile \,|\, - >$$
"quis tibi, saeve puer, dedit hōc in carmina jūris?

$$\smile \smile \; \smile \,|\, - \; \; - \,|\, - \,\|\, - \; \smile\smile \,|\, - \; \; \smile \; \smile \,|\, >$$
Pīeridum vātēs,   nōn tua, turba sumus.

$$- \; \; - \,|\, - \; \smile \smile \,|\, - \; - \,|\, - \; \smile \; \smile \,|\, - \; \smile \; \smile \,|\, - >$$
quid, sī praeripiat flāvae Venus arma Minervae,

$$- \; \smile \; \smile \,|\, - \; - \,|\, - \,\|\, - \; \smile \; \smile \,|\, - \; \; \smile \; \smile \,|\, >$$
ventilet accensās   flāva Minerva facēs?

$$- \; \; \smile \; \smile \,|\, - \; \; - \,|\, \smile \; \smile \; \smile \,|\, - \; \; - \,|\, \; - \; \smile \; \smile \,|\, - >$$
quis probet in silvīs Cererem regnāre jugōsīs,

$$- \; \smile \; \; \smile \,|\, - \; - \,|\, - \,\|\, - \; \smile\smile \,|\, - \; \smile\smile \,|\, >$$
lēge pharētrātae   virginis arva colī? . . ."

(Ovid, *Amores*, bk. 1)

[I was preparing to speak of violence and wars in a serious verse form, the material appropriate to the means. The second verse was equal; but they say Cupid laughed and took away a foot. "Who gave you jurisdiction in this song, savage boy? We are a priest of the muses, not in your crowd. So, if Venus steals the arms of golden Minerva, golden Minerva will brandish the burning torches? Who tells Ceres to rule in the mountainous forests? or to cultivate fields according to the quiver-toting virgin? . . ."]

E.2. Sapphics

$$\_ \ \smile \_ \ \_ \ \_ \ \smile \ \smile \ \_ \ \smile \ \_ >$$
lingua sed torpet, tenuis sub artūs
$$\_ \ \smile \_ \ \_ \_ \ \smile \ \smile \_ \ \smile \ \_>$$
flamma dīmānat, sonitū suopte
$$\_ \ \smile \_ \ \_ \_ \ \smile \ \smile \_ \ \smile \ \_ >$$
tintinant aurēs, geminā teguntur
$$\_ \ \smile \smile \ \_ >$$
lūmina nocte.

(Catullus 51)

―――

[But my tongue is tied, and a tender flame runs through my limbs; my ears ring with a sudden sound and my eyes are covered with twin night.]

E.3. Asclepiads
Asclepiad III:

$$\_ \ \_ \ \_ \smile \ \smile \_ \ \smile \_$$
Dōnec grātus eram tibī,

$$\_ \ \_ \ \_ \ \smile \ \smile \_ \ \_ \ \smile\smile \ \_ \ \smile \_$$
Nec quisquam potior bracchia candidae
$$\_ \ \_\_ \ \smile \smile \_ \ \smile >$$
Cervīcī juvenis dabat,

$$\_ \ \_ \ \_ \ \smile \smile \_ \_ \smile \ \smile \_ \smile >$$
Persārum viguī rēge beātior.

(Horace, *Odes* 3.9)

―――

[When you loved me, no better man placed his arms on your lovely neck, and I lived more blessed than the King of Persia.]

Asclepiad V:

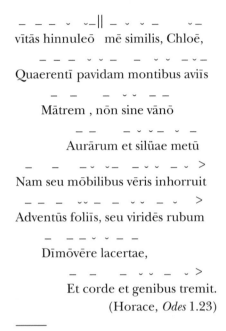

_ _ _ ᵕ ᵕ_‖ _ ᵕ ᵕ _   ᵕ_
vītās hinnuleō mē similis, Chloē,

_ _ _ ᵕ ᵕ _ _ ᵕ ᵕ _ᵕ
Quaerentī pavidam montibus aviīs

_ _ _ ᵕ ᵕ _ _
Mātrem , nōn sine vānō

_ _   _ ᵕ ᵕ _ ᵕ _
Aurārum et silüae metū

_ _ _ᵕ ᵕ_ _ᵕᵕ _ ᵕ >
Nam seu mōbilibus vēris inhorruit

_ _ _ ᵕᵕ _ _ ᵕᵕ _ ᵕ >
Adventūs foliīs, seu viridēs rubum

_ _ _ ᵕ ᵕ _ _
Dīmōvēre lacertae,

_ _ _ ᵕ ᵕ _ ᵕ >
Et corde et genibus tremit.

(Horace, *Odes* 1.23)

———

[You avoid me like a young deer, seeking its fearful mother in the pathless mountains, not without empty fear of the winds and woods. Now in the rustling of spring leaves she fears something approaching, or the green lizards move the blackberry, and she trembles in her heart and knees.]

E.4. Alcaic

_ _ ᵕ _ _ _ ᵕ ᵕ _ ᵕ _
Parcus deōrum cultor et infrequēns

_ _ ᵕ _ _ _ ᵕ ᵕ _ ᵕ_
Insānientis dum sapientiae

_ _ ᵕ _ _ _ ᵕ _ _
Consultus errō, nunc retrōrsum

_ ᵕ ᵕ _ ᵕ ᵕ_ ᵕ _ _
Vēla dare atque iterāre cursūs

‿ ‿ ˘ ‿ ‿ ‿ ˘ ˘‿ ˘ >

Cōgor relictōs: namque Diēspiter,

‿ ‿ ˘ ‿ ‿ ‿ ˘ ˘ ‿ ˘ ‿

Ignī coruscō nūbila dīvidens

‿ ‿ ˘ ‿ ˘ ‿ ˘ ‿ ‿

Plērumque, per purum tonāntēs

‿ ˘ ˘ ‿ ˘ ˘ ‿ ˘ ‿ ‿

Ēgit equōs volucremque currum . . .

(Horace, *Odes* 1.34)

———

[I took little and infrequent account of the gods, when I wandered in foolish wisdom; now I am driven to shift sail and to revisit abandoned courses. For Jupiter, dividing the clouds with blazing fire, drove his thundering horses and winged chariot through the air . . .]

F.2. Iambic Senarius

Modern editions of Roman dramatists rarely if ever mark long vowels but often provide accents on the principal ictus of the first, third, and fifth feet:

> quam plúrimis et mínume multos laédere.

The full scansion of this line is more intelligible with the long vowels marked.

‿   ‿|˘ ‿|‿ ˘ ˘ |‿ ‿|‿ ‿ | ˘ >
quam plūrimīs et minumē multōs laedere

The editorial accent on *min-* indicates the ictus of the iambic foot 3. Here, the basic iambic foot (˘ ‿) has a long in place of the first short; the second long (the element that receives the ictus in an iambic foot) has been resolved as two shorts.

‿ ‿ | ‿ ‿ |˘ ‿|˘ ‿| ˘ ˘ ‿|˘ ‿
Si quisquamst quī placēre sē studeat bonīs
‿   ‿|˘ ‿| ‿ ˘ ˘ ˘| ‿ ‿ |‿ ‿| ˘ >
quam plūrimīs et minumē multōs laedere
˘ ‿|˘ ‿ |‿ ‿| ‿ ˘ ˘ ˘|‿‿| ˘ >
in hīs poēta hīc nōmen profitētur suom

‒ ‒ | ˘ ‒|‒ ‒ | ‒ ‒| ˘ ‒| ˘ >
tum sī quis est quī dictum in sē inclementius
˘ ‒| ˘ ‒ |˘ ‒ | ‒ ‒ |‒ ‒ | ˘ >
existumārit esse, is sīc existumet
‒ ‒ | ‒   ‒ | ‒   ‒| ˘ ˘ ˘|‒ ‒ | ˘ >
responsum, nōn dictum esse, quia laesit prior . . .

                    (Terence, Prologue to *Eunuchus*)

———

[If there is anyone who tries to please good men, however
few, and hurt many the least, among these let the poet place
his name. Then if there is anyone who believes himself to
be roughly treated here, let him have this response . . .]

Chapter 3: Syllabic Verse
C.2.1. Decasyllable (with classical caesura following accented syllable 4):

> Mon dieu terrien ‖ est et fu et sera
> Tant comme en moi ‖ sera vie et nature,
> Et aprés mort ‖ mon ame l'amera
> Pour sa biauté, ‖ qui en envoiseüre
> Nourist mon cuer ‖ de si douce pasture
> Que ne la puet ‖ guerpir n'entroublier,
> Ne qu'on porroit ‖tarir la haute mer.
>   (Guillaume de Machaut,
>   "De mon vrai cuer jamais ne partira")

———

[(Your image) is, was, and will be my earthly god, as long as
in me there will be life and nature; and after death, my soul
will love her for her beauty, which nourished my heart with
such sweet grain, that it could no more abandon or forget
her than one could dry the high sea.]

C.2.3. Decasyllable (with lyric caesura at line 4):

> Princes, qui est ‖ courroussez et pensis
> Voist gens veoir ‖ qui sont a table mis:
> Mieulx ne porra ‖ sa tristesse laissier;

Des grimaces || sera tous esbahis
Que chascun fait; || j'en fu la bien servis:
Oncques ne vis || gens ainsi requignier.
　(Eustaches Deschamps, L'envoy from
　"Tristes, pensis, mas et mornes estoye")

———

[Prince, he who is sad and pensive, let him see people
sitting at his table, there is nothing better to cure his
sadness. He will be amazed at the faces each makes.
I was well served of it; I never saw such grimacers.]

C.3. Classical Alexandrine (caesura marked, alternating masculine
and feminine rhymes):

Il n'est valet d'auteur, || ni copiste à Paris,
Qui la balance en main, || ne pèse les écrits.
Dès que l'impression || fait éclore un poète,
Il est esclave-né || de quiconque l'achète.
Il ne soumet lui-même || aux caprices d'autrui,
Et ses écrits tout seuls || doivent parler pour lui.
Un auteur à genoux, || dans une humble préface,
Au lecteur qu'il ennuie || a beau demander grâce;
　　　　　　　(Boileau, "Son Esprit," Satire 9)

———

[There is no author's valet or copyist in Paris who does not
weigh his words on a scale. As soon as print hatches a poet,
he is a born slave to whoever buys him. He does not submit
himself to another's caprice, and his words must speak for
themselves alone. An author on his knees, does well in his
humble preface to ask for grace from the reader he bores.]

C.4.1. Ternary Alexandrine

Pour la pièce, / elle était fort bonne, / quoique ancienne,
C'était, / nonchalamment assis / sur l'avant-scène
Pierrot, / qui haranguait / dans un grave entretien,
Un singe timbalier / à cheval / sur un chien.
　　　　　　　(Victor Hugo, "La Fête chez Thérèse")

———

[As for the play, it was very good, although old; there was, in
the prologue, sitting nonchalantly, Pierrot, who harangued,
in a grave aside, a performing ape, on horseback, on a dog.]

All have classical caesura following syllable 6. This corresponds to the
presumed *coupe* in lines 3 and 4 but not in lines 1 and 2. I mark the
caesurae in the transcription below:

> Pour la pièce, elle était ‖ fort bonne, quoique ancienne,
> C'était, nonchalamment ‖ assis sur l'avant-scène
> Pierrot, qui haranguait ‖ dans un grave entretien,
> Un singe timbalier ‖ à cheval sur un chien.

Chapter 4: Accentual Verse

In my scansion, I account for all syllables. Syllables that seem to ob-
scure the basic metrical pattern of the line are put (arbitrarily) in
parentheses:

		Sievers's Half-Line Type	
x x X S x X x X x		C	A
Swā ic mōdsefan mīnne sceolde,			
x X S x X x x X x		C	A
oft earmcearig, ēðle bidǣled,			
X S x X X x x X x		E	A
frēomǣgum feor feterum sǣlan,			
x x X x X X x x X x		B	A
siþþan gēara īu goldwine mīnne			
X (x) X x x S x x X X x		D2¹	C
hrūsan heolster biwrāh, and ic hēan þonan			
X X x S x x x X x x x X		D1	B
wōd wintercearig ofer waþema gebind,			
X (x) X(x) S x X x X x		D1	A
sōhte sele drēorig sinces bryttan,			

---

1. In D2-type half-lines, the basic form is X X x S; here and in the lines
below, a short syllable follows the principal stress.

```
x   x  X  x x  X      X x  X  x        B    A
hwær ic feor oþþe nēah   findan meahte
x    x x   X (x) X x      X x  X x        C    A
þone þe in meoduhealle²  minne wisse,
x   x   x   X     S x     X x  X x        C    A
oþþe mec frēondlēasne   frēfran wolde,
X x x   x   X x                           A
wenian mid wynnum.
```

("The Wanderer")

[Thus, I seal with fetters my spirit, often burdened with
cares, bereft of my homeland, far from kinsmen, since long
ago, I buried my goldlord in the earth, and I wandered from
there, winter-weary over the binding of waves, and sorrowing
of home, sought the hall of a giver of treasure, where I far or
near might find in a meadhall him who knew of my kinsmen,
or might comfort me, friendless, cheer with pleasures.]

For source texts see references in chapters 2–4.

------

2. *Meodu-* has two short syllables, here the equivalent of one long; the basic
form is thus x X S x, a C-type half-line.

Glossary of Commonly Used Terms

ACCENT: (1) word accent: the naturally stressed element of any word; (2) verse accent: the metrical stress or *ictus* in a metrical foot.

AEOLIC VERSE: Greek lyric verse forms borrowed by Latin poets; forms include Sapphics, Asclepiadic verse, and Aeolic stanzas (chap. 2, E).

ALEXANDRINE: in French, a twelve-syllable line with caesura following accented syllable 6.

ALLITERATION: the repetition of an initial consonant or vowel. Used as a structural principle in early Germanic verse.

ANACRUSIS: extra-metrical elements preceding an initial foot. Often used in the discussion of Old English. See chap. 4, B.2.1.1.

ARSIS: (1) in Greek, the raising of the foot while marching, thus, the upbeat or light element in a metrical foot; (2) in Latin, the raising of the *voice* in a metrical foot, thus the downbeat or heavy element in a metrical foot; (3) in Old English metrics, the metrical stress, thus the downbeat. See discussion, chap. 2, B.3.2, note 3.

ASCLEPIADIC VERSE: system of lyric verse types in four-line stanzas used by Horace (chap. 2, E.3; appendix).

ASSONANCE: the repetition of a vowel or vowel group at the end of a line in the formation of stanzas. Used as a structural principle in early French epic verse (chap. 3, E).

BLANK VERSE: generally described as unrhymed iambic pentameter.

BREVIS BREVIANS: in Latin dramatic verse, a normally long vowel is shortened if preceded in the word by a short vowel and preceded or followed by a syllable receiving word accent. Thus *benē* could be scanned as ˘ ˘; see chapter 2, A.1d.

BREVIS IN LONGO: in Latin scansion, the substitution of a short syllable for a long at the end of a line: such positions are marked >.

BRIDGE: in Latin verse, a metrical position where word-ending is avoided.

CAESURA: (1) a word break that does not correspond with the break between metrical feet; opposed to *diaeresis* (chap. 2, B.2.2); (2) the regular placement of such a word break in classical verse: in dactylic hexameter, generally in the third foot (chap. 2, D.1.3); (3) A major syntactic and rhythmic break: (a) in classical French Alexandrines, after the sixth position (dividing the line into 6/6); in decasyllables, after the fourth (dividing the line 4/6) (see discussion, chap. 3, B.2); (b) in English verse, often after the fourth or fifth syllable of a ten-syllable line; see discussion, chap. 6, B.

CANTICA: choral sections in Latin drama, often with no repeating metrical element.

CATALEXIS: case where last foot or metron is shorter by a syllable or more. Thus a trochaic tetrameter might consist of four trochaic feet or metra; in catalectic trochaic tetrameter, the last foot would consist only of a single long rather than a long and a short.

CHORIAMB: in quantitative verse, the verse unit ˍ ˘ ˘ ˍ.

COLON (PL. COLA): in classical metrics, a compositional unit of a single, repeatable metrical phrase (chap. 2, B.1.5); for example, the *hemiepes* (half-line) of the pentameter of an elegiac couplet (chap. 2, D.2), or the *glyconic* in Aeolic verse (chap. 2, E).

COUPE: break. Originally used in treatises on French verse as the equivalent of caesura. Now used particularly of Alexandrine verse to refer to breaks between syntactic units of particular lines (chap. 3, D).

DACTYLIC HEXAMETER: in quantitative verse, a line of six dactylic feet with conventional substitutions permitted (chap. 2, D.1; appendix).

DECASYLLABLE: ten-syllable line.

DIAERESIS: (1) in classical hexameter, a break whereby word break corresponds to foot break (chap. 2, B.2.2); (2) in linguistics, the pronunciation of two adjacent vowels as two syllables rather than a diphthong (chap. 3, A.3.2.1).

DIPHTHONG: a combination of two or more vowels that is prosodically understood as a single syllable.

DISTICH: two-line unit in verse.

ELEGIAC COUPLET: in Latin, a couplet consisting of a dactylic hexameter followed by a pentameter (chap. 2, D.2 and appendix; English imitations, chap. 6, A.3).

ELISION: in verse, the metrical dropping of a final syllable ending with a vowel (or certain vowel-consonant combinations) when followed by a word with initial vowel (chap. 2, A.2.1; chap. 3, A.6)

ENJAMBMENT: in French verse, the completion of a syntactic unit in the preceding or following line (chap. 3, D.3).

ENVOY: in medieval French verse, the concluding stanza of a *ballade*, often addressing the poem to a particular listener.

EPIC CAESURA: in French, a caesura following an unaccented syllable whereby that syllable is disregarded in the scansion (chap. 3, C.1.2).

EPODE: (1) a classical form in two-line units employing different verse types or verse bases for each line (chap. 2, G); (2) the third stanza of a three stanza ode, where the first two stanzas have the same form (chap. 5, B.2.2).

GLIEDER (SING. GLIED): verse units occasionally used in the description of early Germanic verse; *Glieder* are the basic units of a foot (chap. 4, B.2.1).

GLYGONIC: verse form x x _ ⌣ ⌣ _ _ ⌣ _ (chap. 2, B.1.5; E.1).

HEMIEPES: the half line unit forming the second line of an elegiac couplet (chap. 2, D.2).

HEMISTICH: half-line. Generally used of the two six-syllable half-lines forming a classical French Alexandrine (chap. 3, B.2.3).

HENDECASYLLABLE: eleven-syllable line; (1) in Italian, this is a basic form; it is equivalent to the French decasyllable, in that both are defined by a terminal accent on syllable 10 (chap. 3, B.2.2.1); (2) for classical form, see chapter 2, E.1.

HEROIC COUPLET: in standard descriptions of English meter, considered rhyming pairs of iambic pentameter. But see proposed scansion in chapter 6, B.1.

HIATUS: a break between elements subject to elision; see chapter 2, A.2.2 (Latin) and chapter 3, A.6.2 (French).

ICTUS: the so-called "heavy" element of a foot or metron; (1) in quantitative verse, the long syllable of a foot (the first syllable of a dactylic foot, the last of an iambic foot); (2) in English, the stressed syllable of these feet.

ISOSYLLABLISM: in the strictest sense, the principle that lines are defined by the number of syllables only, without regard to quantity or accent.

LOGAOEDIC VERSE: term once used by classicists to describe verse that mixes iambic/trochaic and dactylic elements, or spoken and sung forms. No longer used in most discussions of meter.

LYRIC CAESURA: a caesura following an unaccented syllable where this syllable counts as any other syllable (chap. 3, C.1.3).

MEASURE: sometimes used as analogous to the musical foot (chap. 5, A.2.1); in French, often refers to units of phrasal elements making up a particular line (chap. 3, D.1).

MUTE: type of consonant also called a "stop"; in Western phonetics, three groups: unvoiced (*p, t, k*); voiced (*b, d, g*); and aspirate (*f, th, h*). For the effect on determination of syllable quantity in classical languages, see chapter 2, A.1c(2).

ODE: (1) Horatian: lyric verse, generally in four-line stanzas, in specific imitation of Horace (chap. 2, E.2–4); (2) English or romantic ode: stanzaic verse modelled after odes of Pindar (chap. 5, B.2).

PROSODY: the study of the metrical value of particular words and linguistic elements.

QUATRAIN: four-line unit.

RESOLUTION OR RESOLVED SYLLABLE: the substitution of two short syllables for one long (found in Latin and in early Germanic verse).

RHYME RICHE: rhyme that incorporates one more phonetic element than what is required for "sufficient rhyme" (chap. 3, F.1.1).

RHYTHM: a pattern of repeating elements; rhythm is generally a matter of stylistics but can be discussed on the level of versification as well (chap. 3, D.2; chap. 5, A.2.2).

RONDEAU: French fixed form; see chapter 3, G.3.

SAPPHIC STANZA: four-line lyric form used by Sappho in Greek and imitated by Catullus and Horace in Latin (chap. 2, E.2; English imitations, chap. 6, A.4).

SENARIUS: a line consisting of seven metrical feet; used also to refer specifically to the iambic senarius (chap. 2, F.2; appendix).

SONNET: in English, fourteen-line poem in decasyllables, organized into two quatrains and two tercets (Petrarchan), or three quatrains and concluding couplet (Shakespearean).

SPRUNG RHYTHM: a metrical system invented and presumably followed by Gerard Manley Hopkins (chap. 6, C).

STICHIC VERSE: classical term for any verse type involving repeating elements (such as a distich or stanza).

STYLISTICS: as used in this book, refers to elements of verse that are not part of the organizing or foundational principles of a line.

TERCET: three-line unit.

THESIS: *SEE* ARSIS.

TONIC ACCENT: in French, the final stressed syllable of any word (chap. 3. A.4).

VERSE: as used here, equivalent to typographical "line."

VIRELAI: French fixed form; see chapter 3, G.4.